THE COMPLETE GUIDE TO WEST HIGHLAND WHITE TERRIERS

Vanessa Richie

Publication Data

Vanessa Richie

The Complete Guide to West Highland White Terriers – First edition.

Summary: "Successfully raising a West Highland White Terrier Dog from puppy to old age" – Provided by publisher.

ISBN: 978-1-954288-26-3

[1. West Highland White Terriers – Non-Fiction] I. Title.

This book has been written with the published intent to provide accurate and author-itative information in regard to the subject matter included. While every reasonable precaution has been taken in preparation of this book the author and publisher expressly disclaim responsibility for any errors, omissions, or adverse effects arising from the use or application of the information contained inside. The techniques and suggestions are to be used at the reader's discretion and are not to be considered a substitute for professional veterinary care. If you suspect a medical problem with your dog, consult your veterinarian.

Design by Sorin Rădulescu

First paperback edition, 2021

TABLE OF CONTENTS

Introduction

Though considered a small dog, the West Highland White Terrier has the personality and stamina of a much larger dog. That adorable face hides the personality and ability of a much hardier dog. With a stubby tail and long shaggy hair, Westies often look like living stuffed animals even though their coats are not soft because they needed the wiry coat for digging and being outside throughout the breed's history. Often described as irresistible, this is the kind of dog that most people want in their home: small, loving, and cuddly.

While loving and adorable, the West Highland White Terrier is a hard-working dog, just like every other terrier. Originating in Scotland, they were instrumental in keeping the rodent population down where they lived, but they were also hunters with their people. This has given them a high prey

Photo Courtesy of Roy Poh

drive that means you will need to be very aware of your surroundings when you are outside because your dog is very likely to want to give chase—it's just a part of being a Westie.

Westies are a very close relation to the Scottish Terrier, better known as Scotties. The two breeds actually look incredibly similar, except for their coat colors. Scotties are black, and Westies are white. Though they are both energetic dogs, those short little legs mean that it is pretty easy to work that energy off with a couple of brisk walks. Westies are great at sports, training, and agility, as well as hiking and other activities that don't require additional training.

Those longer coats require daily brushing, and you will notice that the shedding increases during warmer months; Westies can be very prolific shedders when it gets warm. Fortunately, you aren't going to have to bathe them often. In fact, it is largely recommended that you avoid bathing your Westie most of the time because they have what is called a hard coat. The

Photo Courtesy
of Terri Peterson

rest of their grooming is pretty easy, or at least not any more difficult than most other breeds.

One of the things that makes Westies so great is that they don't need to be pampered or treated like they are fragile. While you shouldn't be rough with them, they are hardy, independent dogs. Generally, they are known for being easy to train, with the combination of their intelligence and faithfulness making them eager to please while also picking things up quickly.

Westies' intellect and energy can get them in trouble, so they really aren't a great breed for a more sedentary home. With their history of

Photo Courtesy of Debra Brown

chasing smaller animals, especially rodents, they aren't a great choice for homes with most small animals, but they are usually fine with cats. They are vocal, like most terriers, and they are almost certain to dig up the yard if they aren't monitored when they are outside.

This is a great dog for most families, whether the home has one person or a large family. With a life span between 12 and 16 years, when you bring a Westie into your home, you will have a pretty long time with this adoring, fun-loving companion.

CHAPTER 1

Is the Westie Right for You?

Before getting into the details about Westies, it's a good idea to do a quick assessment to see if it is the right breed for your home. As this breed has an extensive history, Westie personalities are pretty predictable, as is their care and health. Having a pretty good idea of what the dog will be like and how much time you will need to spend taking care of your Westie will help you to better determine if the breed is a good fit for your home. If you have younger children, it is probably best to get a puppy to train him how to get along with your younger children. If you are certain that an adult Westie has been exposed to younger children and is fine with them, then you should be alright bringing the canine into your home. You just want to make sure the adult Westie (or any adult dog) knows how to react to children since younger children aren't as aware of how to pet and play with dogs.

By the end of the chapter, you should be able to determine if you think a Westie is an ideal dog for your situation (usually, they are). You'll also have the information you need to determine whether you want a puppy or an adult. Later chapters will provide the details about why Westies behave the way they do, as well as how to care for and train them.

Important Considerations

"A West Highland White Terrier is full of energy, but can fit in any kind of living situation. They are an active breed with plenty of personality, and while they love being outside and investigating their surroundings, they can also fit well in an apartment or condo setting. They are a compact dog that loves to be the center of attention, so having time for your new puppy is a must."

MELANIE CLARK
Gap Kennels

One of the reasons that people love older breeds is that you pretty much know what you are going to get, regardless of the age of the dog. Socialization can help minimize some behaviors, but older dog breeds are largely set in their traits. Here's what you can expect from your adorable little West Highland White Terrier.

Photo Courtesy of Aubrey Santillo

Element	Description
What's Great About Them	
A Fantastic First Family Dog	If you have never had a dog before, the Westie is a fantastic dog to bring into your home. From their gregarious and enthusiastic nature to their love of being active, they can fit into any busy, active home.
A Good Watch Dog, but not a Good Guard Dog	Just like they used to let their people know where the prey was, your Westie can quickly let you know when there is someone around your home. They aren't particularly aggressive, and with their size, they aren't much of a threat. But the loud, constant barking is definitely something that you can't miss.
A Great Family Dog	Puppies can befriend just about anyone. You will need to be careful with younger children to make sure that they aren't too rough with your dog. However, you can take your Westie out on family trips, and he'll be able to join you for whatever fun you have planned for the day.
Can Help You Make Time for Exercise	This is a breed that will force you off the couch and outside to get some exercise. Some Westies have even joined in for half marathons. Whether you like jogging, hiking, or walking, this is a dog that can help you get out and get moving.
One of the Most Tolerant Terriers	Unlike most terriers, Westies are less wary of strangers and warm up to outsiders much faster. They tend to get along well with other dogs and cats, so they can be a wonderful addition to any family.
Why They May Not Be Right for You	
Separation Anxiety	If you aren't home for much of the day, a Westie may have some trouble adjusting. They aren't particularly prone to separation anxiety if they have someone else in the home, even another dog or a cat, but you will need to be aware of how your dog feels. You should monitor your Westie to make sure he isn't developing this problem.

Inevitability of Shedding	Terriers are shedders—you simply cannot have that much fuzz and not shed—and the Westie is no exception. It will be worse during seasonal changes, but daily brushings can help to significantly reduce this problem.
Potentially Stubborn	Westies are intelligent, but they have to be convinced that they should listen to you. If they don't see what's in something for them, they can really dig their heels in to keep from doing whatever it is you want to do.
Almost certainly vocal	Terriers had to be vocal for centuries, so you are going to be working against a legacy of barking. Plan to train your Westie to be a bit less vocal because barking is a near inevitability with the breed.
An Ardent Digger	If you have a yard, you will not be able to leave your dog outside alone. When unsupervised, Westies can dig holes all over your yard.
Strong Prey Drive	They are more likely to be incredibly aggressive toward small animals, especially rodents and rabbits.
Numerous Health Issues	Terriers (and most older breeds) have a lot of known health problems, and Westies, unfortunately, have a relatively long list of potential health issues.

Adult Versus Puppy

The final question to ask yourself before you settle on a breed is whether you should get an adult or a puppy. The answer varies based on the individual or family. Here are some considerations to help you determine which age dog is a better fit for your home.

Bringing Home an Adult Westie

With a breed like a Westie, you need to be careful about adopting an adult; if the dog is not properly trained, life can turn into a real struggle because of how stubborn they can be. That said, adults can sometimes quickly integrate into your home with very little work on your part.

Photo Courtesy of Angela Venn

If you have young children at home, you will need to watch your dog closely and make sure he has a positive reaction to kids before bringing him home, especially if you don't know the dog's history with children. You will also need to be careful about introducing a Westie to other pets, though most Westies tend to warm up to other animals fairly quickly, unless the animals are smaller, as discussed earlier.

On the positive side, older dogs can give you more immediate gratification. You don't have to go through the sleepless nights that come with a new puppy. The odds are also that you aren't going to be starting from scratch with house training.

Additionally, adult dogs are awake during the day more than puppies, and while it may take your dog a bit longer to warm up to you, you can bond much faster with an adult.

Finally, one of the biggest benefits of acquiring an adult dog is that it will already be its full size. There is no need for guessing how big your dog will grow to be, and that makes it easier to purchase the appropriate-sized gear and supplies right from the start.

The following is a list of questions to consider when adopting an adult Westie:

- Can you properly dog-proof your home before the dog arrives?

You can't simply bring a dog into your home, whether an adult or a puppy, and let him run around unchecked. To be sure he learns the rules of the house before roaming freely, you will need to have a

FUN FACT
West Highland Terrier Club of America (WHWTCA)

The West Highland Terrier Club of America (WHWTCA) is this breed's official American Kennel Club Parent Club. Established in 1909, the WHWTCA sponsors annual shows and supports research for the breed. A quarterly magazine and monthly newsletter are included in the price of membership. For more information about the club and its membership benefits, visit www.westieclubamerica.com.

safe, dedicated space for your new dog. (Details of how to dog-proof your home are discussed in Chapter 6.)

● Do you have pets who will be affected by a new dog?

Westies are likely to get along just fine with any dog—and probably cats—but you will still want to be very careful since you don't know the dog's history with other animals. This introduction should take place over the first couple of months. Introducing the animals in a neutral territory will show you what to expect when your Westie and your current dogs are together on a permanent basis. Even if they appear to be compatible, you still need to keep them apart for a while. This will ensure your new Westie understands that the other dogs are part of the pack and are not a threat to him.

You will need to be aware of how your other dog(s) reacts as well. Even if your current dog is very friendly, you will still want to be careful when introducing the two and allowing them to interact in your home.

● What is the dog's health history?

A complete health record for a rescue Westie may not be available, but it is likely you will find a dog that has already been spayed or neutered as well as chipped. Unless you adopt a Westie with health issues, which should be disclosed by the rescue organization if known, rescues tend to be less costly than puppies at their first vet visit. In other words, for the first few years, your Westie's health-care visits should not be too expensive.

Bringing Home a Westie Puppy

Puppies are a major time investment, and a dog as intelligent and potentially stubborn as the Westie will make some aspects of raising a puppy that much harder. How much time can you devote to a puppy's care? Will you be able to deal with an excitable puppy that has everything to learn?

A puppy will be a better fit if you put in dedicated time for training and socializing before the dog becomes set in his ways. If you have other pets at home, a puppy is definitely a better choice than an adult because he is young and can be trained to follow YOUR rules. (The exception would be if you find an adult that is already well-socialized.)

The following should be considered when determining whether or not a Westie puppy is a good fit for your home:

- How much time do you have available for training and socialization?

All puppies are a lot of work, starting with the moment the puppy enters your care. While the Westie's temperament is fairly predictable, how you train and socialize your puppy will affect every aspect of the dog's adult life. Training and socializing can take up a large chunk of time in the beginning, but both are absolutely essential for raising a healthy Westie.

Photo Courtesy
of Michael and Jennifer Luciano

- Are you able to show firmness and consistency when training such an adorable puppy?

From the very beginning, you have to establish yourself and your family as the ones in charge; your Westie must understand his place in the family hierarchy. You will need to be patient and consistent with your training, no matter how frustrated you become or how cute those puppy eyes appear. All intelligent dogs have a streak of stubbornness!

- Do you have the time, energy, and budget to puppy-proof your home?

The preparation for your puppy's arrival begins long before he first sets foot in your house. Puppy-proofing your home is as time-consuming as child-proofing your home. If you do not have the time for this, then you should consider getting an adult dog instead of a puppy. (Details of how to puppy-proof your home are discussed in Chapter 6.)

What most people love about adopting a puppy is that they will spend more time with a puppy than with an adult dog since the puppy still has its whole life ahead of it. You will receive records about the puppy and the puppy's parents, which will make it easier to identify any problems your Westie might experience in the future. This makes it considerably easier to keep your puppy healthy and to spot potential issues before they become major problems.

Some people find it easier to bond with puppies than with adult dogs. A young puppy may be nervous in a new home, but most adjust quickly because they are predisposed to enjoying the company of those around them.

CHAPTER 2
Breed History of the West Highland White Terrier

The West Highland White Terrier, better known as the Westie, has a long history as a working dog in Scotland, then moving into the wider world as people realized just how amazing the breed was. Hunting in the Scottish terrain where they originated made them an incredibly sturdy breed that is able and willing to do a lot more than just sit around as a charming little lap companion.

Photo Courtesy of Melissa Beckwith

A Family of Scottish Terrier Breeds

The Westie is one of several well-known Scottish terriers bred specifically to deal with the infestations of rodents across the island. England and Wales were also breeding their own dogs to take care of the problem, but terriers tended to be favored because their size helped them to better fit into small areas. This included being able to fit into holes, which terriers widened through digging—something to remember when you are considering whether a Westie is a good breed for your home.

FUN FACT
How Popular Are They?

As of 2021, West Highland White Terriers are the 42nd most popular breed in the United States out of 200 breeds registered with the American Kennel Club (AKC). The AKC first recognized Westies in 1908 as the Roseneath Terrier, but the name was changed to West Highland White Terrier on May 31, 1909. Westies were first shown at Scottish dog shows in 1896.

Popular terrier breeds from Scotland include the following:

- West Highland White Terrier
- Scottish Terrier – best known of all the breeds. With its black coat, rectangular face and body, carrot-shaped tail, and stubby legs, it's easy to see why the Scottie has been such a popular breed for a long time.
- Cairn Terrier – looks similar to the Westie but with a hazel-colored coat. They are known for being cheerful and active, something that is pretty universal for all Scottish Terriers.
- Skye Terriers – look similar to Scotties, but they have a longer body, shorter nose, and longer hair than their better-known Scottish relatives. They are known for being courageous, and their history is thought to have started in the Scottish Hebrides islands.
- Dandie Dinmont – probably the least well-known terrier on the list, and it is distinctively different in appearance from the others. Dandies appear more like a strange variation of a Dachshund with their shorter fur and long bodies. However, their personalities are very much aligned with their other terrier relatives.

It is likely that all of these breeds have the same genetic roots, particularly given how similar their appearance is and the genetic issues that many of them have. Petting a Westie makes it clear that the breed's history is

tied to the outdoors because they have wiry coats that are not soft to the touch. This helped them to keep from getting as dirty since things did not stick to their fur as much. Their coat colors are reflective of the initial colors, including black, red, white, and cream; all of these terriers have variations of these colors today.

A Long History as a Hard Worker

"Westies are watchers and workers. They watch out the window (or watch the TV) for cars, birds, rabbits, squirrels, or chipmunks. They feel the need to alert you if they see something worrisome and a desire to chase it down and catch it if needed."

MARLEEN C BURFORD
MARDOT

A small body, wiry hair, fuzzy face, and recognizable bark were what made the Westie so good at the jobs it was originally given. The dogs weren't that much larger than some of the animals they chased, and if something like a rabbit ran down a hole, the Westie could follow them, digging as needed. Noblemen, farmers, and landowners all had Westies because of how useful the breed was for dealing with small animals. Some of those animals were actually larger than the Westie, such as foxes and badgers. Their tenacity and drive to catch prey were what made them so important within their families.

Taking on these larger and intelligent mammals meant that Westies had to be able to outthink their prey. To be successful, they needed to be able to run quickly and sometimes for long distances, and this is something that they have certainly retained over the centuries, along with their intelligence.

Photo Courtesy
of Letty Zemaitis

Over the centuries, cats and smaller dogs had a lot of work to take care of rodents around homes and farms. They were the primary method of pest control. As a result, when Westies weren't hunting, they had plenty of work to do around their home, especially if they were on a farm and crops needed to be protected. The highlands of Scotland aren't the easiest terrain, which is what has led to the breed having such high stamina.

Breeding by the Malcolm Clan

While Westies' exact history is not known, historians have traced the breed back to the 18th century and the Malcolm clan's Poltalloch estate. Some call the Westie the Poltalloch Terrier because of this. The breed was also called the Roseneath Terrier because some dogs were bred on the Roseneath estate. It is thought that the breed could date back to King James I, who wanted an Argyllshire dog.

The breed also has its own lore related to Colonel Malcolm of Poltalloch. It's said that he accidentally shot one of his dogs while fox hunting. The dog had been a cream-colored Cairn, which allowed it to blend in with the surroundings and, therefore, be more easily confused with the prey they were hunting. To ensure that this kind of tragic accident did not happen again, the colonel is said to have only bred white dogs thereafter.

For the better part of 100 years, Westies continued to be bred, and then they began to make their way to dog shows. When a Westie appeared for the first time in an 1896 Scottish dog show, it was officially given the name the West Highland White Terrier. This referenced the region from which it came instead of the specific estates, though by the end of the1800s, the dogs were also being bred in other places. The breed made its first appearance in the Kennel Club of England show in 1906. In 1908, the breed was registered as the 61st breed recognized by the American Kennel Club. They quickly became an incredibly popular dog in the US after that first show.

CHAPTER 3
West Highland White Terrier Attributes and Temperament

"The Westie is a breed for adults. They thrive at home with seniors, emp-ty nesters or couples. Even though Westies are 'pack' animals, and most think of all people and dogs as potential pack members, there are a few exceptions. Although families with young children can be successful in owning Westies; they are terriers, which means they think a lot of themselves and won't tolerate an overly curious youngster that might push, pinch, pull or prod. But kind-hearted, 'gentle' children are a perfect match. And if you work from home or are retired, the Westie can become your constant companion to your mutual benefit."

BONNIE SUE HURLEY
OakTree Kennels

Westies are considered small dogs, weighing between 13 and 19 pounds, or 6 to 8.5 kg, and standing between 10 to 11 inches, or 25 to 28 cm, tall. However, you can't let that small frame fool you. This is a breed that is both remarkably sturdy and incredibly agile. Unlike their close relative, the Scottie, when you see a Westie, you could mistake the pup for one of several other terrier breeds. However, the personality is a very easy way of knowing that you are dealing with a Westie.

FUN FACT
Hypoallergenic or Not?

West Highland White Terriers are low-shedding dogs who are usually considered a hypoallergenic breed, meaning that the amount of dander is lower with this breed. No dog is entirely hypoallergenic, but Westies may be less likely to induce an allergic response than a high-shedding breed. In addition, regular brushing and grooming can help remove any loose hair and further reduce the amount of dander in the home.

The Stereotypical Terrier

From the very distinctive wiry hair to the short tail to the sturdy body, it's easy to quickly identify this cutie as a terrier.

SMALL, STURDY PUP

Westies aren't very big, not even coming up to most adult's knees. The males tend to be slightly larger than the females, but it's not enough of a disparity to be noticeable. The rectangular body is what helps to make the breed so sturdy. They are small and compact, with some impressive leg muscles hidden under all of that fuzz.

ADORABLE, WIZENED FACE

Whether well-groomed or otherwise, Westies have that typical wizened terrier face. The face is nearly perfectly round, especially if you get the hair around the face cut in that style. The dark eyes hidden behind the hair that is around the face have an alert and knowledgeable look to them. This is emphasized by the small triangular ears that stand up when the dog is interested in hearing what you have to say.

THE TERRIER COAT

Westies have double coats, which means they need a lot of grooming. They also have a combination of fur and hair, which makes it more interesting to tend their fur. Their coat is coarse and long, and since it is white, it shows off dirt and mud very easily. This is why many people prefer to have a professional groomer give Westies a regular trim—it keeps the dogs looking cleaner. Chapter 15 provides more detail about how to properly care for your Westie's coat.

Photo Courtesy of Jolyn Zimmermann

Temperament

"Westies are very confident. They're big dogs in little dogs' bodies. They're not mean, but they can be assertive, so they're best suited for families that can offer structure and consistency with training."

FRANCES ROBERSON
Nancy's Westies

What really makes Westies different from many other terriers (and the stereotypical idea of a small breed) is that they tend to be fairly sociable, aren't demanding, and are very independent. They learn quickly, but they need a reason to listen to you.

A BIG DOG IN A SMALL BODY

This isn't a needy breed that will be constantly looking for your attention. Your dog will be able to think about the situation and make decisions because that was what his ancestors had to do while working in the Highlands. Yes, your Westie is likely to want to play with you, but he's not going to be eager to please. He'll want both a challenge and a good dose of exercise. This is what makes activities like agility training and obedience competitions exceptionally good for this breed.

FRIENDLY, FAITHFUL, AND LOYAL

Even though a Westie is more likely to want to know what he will get out of listening to you, as long as you are firm and consistent, you'll find your Westie can quickly learn the value in listening. Loyalty toward the family is something that has been an important part of the breed's lives for centuries. They are accustomed to being companions, so they know how to entertain and play with the people they spend their time with. Even if your Westie does end up having a favorite person, he isn't the kind of dog that will just stick to one person. Surprisingly, Westies are usually even friendly with strangers.

INTELLIGENT AND EASY TO TRAIN

You should keep in mind that a Westie is intelligent because your dog can cause you a lot of problems if you don't keep him from getting bored. As long as you can convince your Westie that training to do tricks is a fun activity, you'll find that it does not take that long to get him to do the most common tricks, and then you can move into the more entertaining and complicated tricks, like dancing and jumping.

Photo Courtesy
of Anna Liza Groat

This is a dog that can easily stun visitors with just how agile and capable he is and how many different tricks he can do. If you decide to get a Westie, you are going to have a dog that can be quite the little entertainer at parties.

GREAT TRAVEL COMPANION

Since Westies are generally a friendly, fun-loving breed, they make absolutely fantastic travel companions. As small dogs, they will be allowed to stay in a lot more places than larger canines. They also don't require much room in your vehicle when you travel. With their high energy levels, they'll be able to keep up with you while you explore. And when you get home, they'll be just as happily tired as you.

By taking your Westie with you, even to run errands or spend time at a park, you'll make him incredibly happy. It's a great way to keep your pup from getting bored and use up some of that energy on the excitement of leaving home—even if only for a couple of hours.

A PREFERENCE FOR CLEANLINESS

Westies prefer a clean living space, something that will go a long way to helping you crate train your pup. You will need to crate train him, and your Westie puppy shouldn't be allowed to run around your home unless he is being supervised. Given your dog's small size and intelligence, he will be able to hide what he is doing if you don't constantly keep an eye on him until he is fully house trained. Chapter 10 will go into more detail, but just know that house training can be very easy with the right approach.

A HIGH PREY DRIVE

Perhaps one of the biggest downsides to the Westie (at least if you have small animals at home) is a high prey drive. With such an extensive history of chasing down small animals, even on a leash, a Westie can be particularly adamant about chasing any little creature that is unfortunate enough to run in front of him. If you have a problem with small animals in your yard, this could be a great way of keeping them from getting out of control. If there's one thing that will get a Westie excited and agitated, it's a small animal that he thinks he can catch.

Photo Courtesy of Michael and Jennifer Luciano

THE TERRIER LOVE OF BARKING

Since Westies used to bark to help hunters find them during the chase, they have some very robust lungs, coupled with a desire to communicate. This is a dog that will be an incessant barker if you don't train him to be a bit quieter. Don't worry; with the right training and convincing, your Westie can really learn to tone down his barking. Chapter 12 covers different training options, including how to teach vocal dogs to be choosier in when or why they bark. Given their size, they don't make great guard dogs, but with their enthusiasm for barking, Westies do make fantastic watchdogs.

Don't Confuse Them with These Breeds

The dog breeds that have a very similar appearance to the Westie include the following:

- **Bichon Frise,** a fluffy white dog that looks a lot like a toy Poodle or a well-trimmed Westie but is more mellow
- **Maltese,** a small white dog with similar long hair that is often styled; more of a lapdog than an outdoor enthusiast like the Westie.
- **Sealyham Terrier,** probably the most similar-looking breed; nearly as energetic, and their eyes tend to have more hair around them, giving the breed a shaggier appearance
- **Coton De Tulear,** probably the easiest breed to tell apart with the black fur on their ears and fuller bodied hair

Small dogs with white fur are pretty common, but there is no other breed quite like the energetic, fun-loving, fearless, loyal Westie with its large dog personality.

CHAPTER 4

Finding Your West Highland White Terrier

"Research, research, research. Different breeders breed for different characteristics, so figure out what you're wanting in a dog, and find a breeder who specializes in those aspects. Also, make sure to touch base with people who have bought Westies from your breeder. Most reputable breeders will have a social media presence, which offers a fantastic opportunity to network with other owners and find out what kind of operation the breeder runs."

FRANCES ROBERSON
Nancy's Westies

If you've decided this is the right breed for your home, you are in for a real treat because of how much personality is packed into that little Westie body. Deciding which breed you want is just the beginning of a set of decisions you need to make.

Ways to Get a Westie

This chapter is broken into two primary sections: rescuing a Westie and adopting a Westie. Typically, people rescue an adult, and they adopt a puppy.

- Dog rescues are one of the most reliable ways to get an adult Westie who is more likely to be healthy. The rescuers tend to go above and beyond to ensure the health of the dog.

- Shelters are usually rescue places that are not dedicated to any one breed, and as often as not, their dogs are not pure-bred. However, that doesn't mean you can't find a Westie or a dog that has a lot of Westie genetics and that lovable temperament.

Photo Courtesy
of Michele Durbin

While you can get puppies from both of these places, it is more likely that you will find a puppy at one of the following sources:

- Breeders are the most reliable source for purebred dogs, but you do have to be careful.

- Puppy mills focus on producing as many dogs as possible for the lowest cost. They are far less likely to do testing and screening, so their dogs are more likely to have genetic problems than puppies from a breeder.

- Pet stores are more of a mixed bag. They may get their dogs from a puppy mill; they aren't likely to get their dogs from a great breeder (breeders who really take care of their dogs are far more likely to be picky about who adopts their puppies).

You can actually find rescued puppies from puppy mills and pet stores at a dog rescue or pet shelter. You can also get a great adult dog from a breeder, especially if a breeder takes one of their dogs back from a client who did not follow the contract. Sometimes people have to surrender their dogs, and breeders often prefer to have their dogs returned so they can find another good home (for example, a family may have to move somewhere that doesn't allow dogs).

This section is really more of a guide to where you are likely to find your Westie. To find your perfect Westie, make sure to check multiple avenues—unless you want a puppy, in which case a breeder is probably your best bet.

Rescuing a West Highland White Terrier

"If you get a Westie from a rescue, you will need to ask about their past history and check on any type of health issues encountered. A Westie is a very habit forming dog and loves a schedule, so any type of previously learned behavior will be hard to change. It can be accomplished, but only with love, patience, and consistency of the new owner."

MELANIE CLARK
Gap Kennels

Photo Courtesy
of Reneé Murphy

Like most popular pure breeds, there are a number of rescues dedicated to the Westie breed. The following are two websites dedicated to helping people find a Westie rescue anywhere in the US:

- Westie Rescue USA (https://westierescue.com)
- Find a Local Westie Rescue (https://westierescue.com/find-a-local-westie-rescue/)

You can also contact Westie breeders to see if they have had any of their puppies returned that are now at least two years old. That way, the breeders will have a better understanding of the dog and its personality, and they will be able to answer any future questions you might have.

Keep in mind the following questions when adopting a Westie:

- What is the reason the dog was surrendered?
- Did the dog have any health issues when he arrived?
- Do they know how the dog was treated by the previous family? What kind of training was he given, was he mistreated, and was he socialized?
- How many homes has the dog experienced?
- What kind of veterinary care did the dog receive? Are there records that confirm this?
- Will the dog require extra medical attention based on known or suspected problems?
- Is the dog house trained?
- How well does the dog react to strangers while walking in unfamiliar areas?
- Does the dog have good eating habits, or does he tend to be more aggressive when eating?
- How does the dog react to children and to other dogs and pets?
- Does the dog have any known allergies?
- Does the dog have any known dietary restrictions?
- If there are problems with the dog after adoption, will the organization take him back?

It is unlikely that you will find a Westie at a shelter. Shelters are rarely certain of the breeds of their dogs because their charges are often abandoned, dropped off, or rescued without any information on genetics. You may get lucky and find a purebred, or more likely, you'll find a dog that has some Westie heritage. Either way, you'll have a dog with some real potential to make your home a lot livelier.

Choosing a West Highland White Terrier Breeder and Puppy

"Chose a good breeder or an established, reputable breed rescue and let them choose the right Westie for you! An experienced breeder spends hours with a litter of puppies every day. The breeder will do early neurological stimulation and temperament testing and judge the personality and activity level of each puppy. You cannot possibly spend an hour or two and 'pick' the best puppy for your situation. Tell your breeder or rescue as much as possible about your lifestyle and expectations for your puppy and rely on their judgment to choose the perfect puppy for you."

BONNIE SUE HURLEY
OakTree Kennels

Finding a responsible breeder is the best thing you can do for your puppy because good breeders work only with healthy Westie parents, which reduces the odds of serious health issues.

Always take the time to do your research before moving forward. You can start with breeders in surrounding areas in your state or research sites that are strictly dedicated to the breed. Although breeders for Westies are largely reputable, you also might run across an individual who is more interested in making a lot of money than in caring for his dogs.

The goal is to locate breeders who are willing to answer ALL of your questions patiently and thoroughly. They should show as much love for their Westies as they expect you to show for your new puppy; their goal should be to locate good homes for all of their animals.

It is a particularly good sign if you find a breeder who posts pictures and information about the dog's parents, documents the progress of the mother's pregnancy, and shares descriptions of all vet visits. The best breeders will also stay in contact with you and answer any questions that might arise after you take the puppy home. These are also breeders who are likely to have waiting lists. Taking an active interest in what happens to the puppies in their new home shows that they care a great deal about each individual dog.

You also want to find a breeder who is willing to talk about problems that might develop with your Westie. Good breeders will ensure the adopting family is capable of properly socializing and training their Westie since both of these activities are essential as a puppy matures.

29

Photo Courtesy
of Margaret Meroni

It is likely that your conversation with each breeder will last about an hour. Make sure you take careful notes during every interview. If a breeder does not have time to talk when you call and isn't willing to call you back— cross them off your list!

The following are some questions to consider when researching breeders:

- Ask if you can visit in person. The answer should always be yes, and if it isn't, you don't need to ask anything further. Thank the breeder and hang up. Even if the breeder is located in a different state, they should always allow you to visit their facility.

- Ask about the required health tests and certifications breeders have for their puppies. (These points are detailed further in the next section, so make sure to check off the available tests and certifications with every breeder.) If they don't have all of the tests and certifications, remove the breeder from your list of considerations.

- Make sure the breeder takes care of the initial health requirements, particularly shots, for each puppy—from the first few weeks of birth through the dog's early months. Puppies require certain procedures before they leave their mother in order to ensure they are healthy. Vaccinations and worming typically start at around six weeks of age and should be continued every three weeks. By the time your puppy is old enough to come home with you, he should be well into the first phase of these procedures or completely finished with these important health care needs.

- Ask if the puppy is required to be spayed or neutered before reaching a certain age.

- Inquire whether or not the breeder is part of a Westie organization or group.

- Ask about the first phases of your puppy's life, such as how the breeder takes care of the puppy prior to its going home with you. They should be able to provide a lot of details, and they should not sound irritated by your questioning. They should also explain what training your puppy will receive prior to leaving the facility. It is possible the breeder might start house training your puppy. If so, ask about the puppy's progress so that you know where to pick up training once your Westie reaches your home.

- Breeders should be more than happy to help guide you in doing what is best for your dog because they should want their puppies to live happy, healthy lives. You should also be able to rely on any recommendations your breeder makes about taking your puppy home, particularly about the first days with the puppy.

Photo Courtesy of Irene Kenny

- Ask how many varieties of dogs the breeder manages in one year and how many sets of parent dogs they own. Mother dogs should have some downtime between pregnancies before producing another litter. Learn about the breeders' standard operations to be sure they take care of the parents and treat them like valuable family members—not strictly as a way to make money.

- Ask about aggression in the puppy's parents and find out if there are other dogs in the breeder's home. While a puppy's temperament is more malleable than an adult's, some exposure to other breeds might make it easier when integrating him into a home that already has dogs. Aggression isn't a normal problem for Westies, but if you have smaller animals in your home, this will be important to know.

Contracts and Guarantees

Breeder contracts and guarantees are meant to protect the puppies as much as they are meant to protect you. If a breeder has a contract, make sure you read through it completely and are willing to meet all of the requirements prior to signing. Contracts tend to be fairly easy to understand and to comply with, but you should be aware of all the facts before you agree to anything. Signing the contract indicates you are serious about committing to giving your puppy the best care possible and to meeting the minimum care requirements set forth by the breeder.

A contract may state the breeder will retain the puppy's original registration papers, although you will receive a copy of the papers, too.

If a family does not meet all requirements as stated in the contract, it is the breeder's responsibility to remove that puppy from the family. These are the dogs some breeders offer for adoption.

A guarantee states the kind of health care the breeder's puppy is to receive once it leaves

FUN FACT
A Coat of Many Colors

West Highland White Terriers were not always white! In the early days of this hunting breed, the dogs' fur could range from white to red to black to cream. How the Westie came to be ubiquitously white isn't known for sure, but it's believed that Colonel Edward Donald Malcolm was the man who brought this change about. The story goes that one of Malcolm's red-coated hunting dogs was mistaken for a fox on a hunting expedition and shot, at which point he decided to breed only white dogs who would be easily identified in the field.

the breeder's facility. This typically includes details about the dog's current health and the recommendations for the next steps in the puppy's health care. Guarantees may also provide veterinary schedules to ensure that the health care started by the breeder is continued by the new puppy parent. In the event that a major health concern surfaces, the puppy will be returned to the breeder.

The contract will also explain what is not covered by the guarantee. A guarantee tends to be quite long (sometimes longer than the contract), and you should also read it thoroughly before the signing.

Westie contracts usually include a requirement that the dog be spayed or neutered once it reaches maturity (typically six months). The contract may also contain requirements for naming your puppy (if you would like more information about naming requirements, check out the American Kennel Club for details about contracts), details of the puppy's health, and a stipulation regarding what will happen if you can no longer take care of the animal. (The dog is usually returned to the breeder.) Information concerning the steps that will be taken if the new owner is negligent or abusive to the dog is also included in the contract.

Health Tests and Certifications

A healthy puppy requires healthy parents and a clean genetic history, which is a bit more difficult to guarantee in a Westie due to the lengthy history of this breed. A breed with so many potential genetic issues (you can check out the potential genetic problems in Chapter 17), like the Westie, needs a breeder who seriously follows good breeding practices. A conscientious breeder keeps extensive records for each puppy and its parents. You should review each of the parents' complete histories to understand what traits your puppy is likely to inherit. Pay attention to temperament, learning traits, attachment issues, and any other personality traits you consider important. You can request these documents be sent to you electronically, or you can pick them up when you visit the breeder in person.

It might be time-consuming to review the breeder's information for each parent, but it is always well worth the time. The more you know about the parents, the better prepared you will be for your puppy.

All breeders should ensure their Westies undergo the following health tests:

- Hip Evaluation
- Ophthalmologist Evaluation
- Patella Evaluation

Selecting a Puppy from a Breeder

"Just because a puppy or rescue appears to be 'the one', be it because they came running to you, licked your hand or made eye contact doesn't mean they are the best choice for your family. If you are taking a new family member home from a reputable breeder work with them to understand each puppies personality and how they may match your family and lifestyle."

CHRISTOPHER LARSON
West Highland White Terrier

Selecting your puppy should be done in person. However, if the breeder is willing to share videos and pictures, you can start checking out your puppy immediately after he is born!

You should consider the following steps once you are allowed to visit the puppy in person:

- Assess the group of puppies as a whole. If most or all of the puppies are aggressive or fearful, this is an indication of a problem with the litter or (more likely) the breeder. The following are considered red flags if they are displayed by a majority of the puppies:
  - Tucked tails
  - Shrinking away from people
  - Whimpering when people get close
  - Constant attacking of your hands or feet (beyond pouncing)
- Notice how each puppy plays with the other puppies in the litter. This is a great indicator of how your puppy will react to any pets you already have at home. If you see problems with the way one puppy plays, this could be a problem later.
- Notice which puppies greet you first and which puppies hang back to observe you from afar. This lets you know their personality and how likely they are to be laid back later.
- Puppies should not be over or underweight. A swollen stomach is generally a sign of worms or other health problems.
- Puppies should have straight, sturdy legs. Splayed legs can be a sign that there is something wrong.
- Examine the puppy's ears for mites, which will cause a discharge if present. The inside of the ear should be pink, not red or inflamed.

35

- The eyes should be clear and bright.
- Check the puppy's mouth for pink, healthy-looking gums.
- Pet the puppy to check his coat for the following:
  - Be sure the coat feels thick and full. If breeders have allowed puppies' fur to get matted or dirty, it is an indication they are likely not taking proper care of the animals.
  - Check for fleas and mites by running your hand from the head to the tail; then check under the tail as fleas are more likely to hide under a dog's tail. If mites are present, they may look like dandruff.
- Check the puppy's rump for redness and sores; try to check the puppy's last bowel movement to ensure its firmness.

Pick the puppy that exhibits the personality traits you want in your dog. If you want a forward, friendly, excitable dog, the first puppy to greet you may be the one you choose. If you want a dog that will think things through and let others get more attention, look for a puppy that sits back and observes before approaching you. That initial reaction should be on the puppy's terms as much as your own so that you can determine if the personality matches what you think will fit best in your home.

CHAPTER 5

Preparing Your Budget and Family for Your New Westie

Preparing to bring home an intelligent dog is always a unique challenge. There is a lot to do to prepare, regardless of if you bring home an adult or a puppy.

Photo Courtesy
of Abigail Orenstein

Planning the First Year's Budget

Whether you get a puppy or an adult dog, the costs are always higher than you initially think, or even the second or third thought. You will definitely want a budget, which is a good reason to start purchasing supplies a few months in advance. When you buy the items you need, you will begin to formulate an idea of how much money you will spend each month. Many of these items are one-time purchases (or won't need to be bought too often, like a bed), but many other items, like food and treats, will have to be purchased regularly.

The following table will help you plan your budget. Keep in mind the prices are rough estimates and may be significantly different based on your location.

Item	Considerations	Estimated Costs
Crate	You may need two crates: one for the home and one for trips to the vet. If you would like, you can have just one crate; it's usually a matter of personal preference. The crate at home should be a comfortable space where the puppy will sleep and rest.	Wire crate: $60 to $350 Portable crate: $35 to $200
Bed	This will be placed in the crate.	$10 to $55
Leash	It should be short in the beginning because you need to be able to keep your puppy from getting overly excited and running to the end of a long line.	Short leash: $6 to $15 Retractable: $8 to $25
Doggie bags for walks	If you walk at dog parks, this won't be necessary. For those who don't have daily access to bags, it is best to purchase packs to ensure you don't run out.	Singles cost less than $1 each. Packs: $4 to $16
Collar	You will need to get a collar that can be loosened over time, but it isn't likely that you will need two different collars. Just make sure you check how tight the collar is as your dog grows up.	$10 to $30

Tags	These will likely be provided by your vet. Find out what information the vet provides for tags; then, purchase any tags that are not provided. At a minimum, your Westie should have a tag with your address on it in case the pup escapes.	Contact your vet before purchasing to see if the required rabies tags include your contact info.
Puppy food	The larger the bag of dog food, the higher the cost, but the fewer times you will need to purchase food. You will need to purchase specific puppy food in the beginning. Adult dog food is more expensive.	$9 to $90 per bag
Water and food bowls	These will need to be kept in the puppy's area. If you have other dogs, you will need separate bowls for the puppy.	$10 to $40
Toothbrush/ Toothpaste	You will need to brush your Westie's teeth regularly, so plan to buy more than one toothbrush during the first year.	$2.50 to $14
Hairbrush	Westie coats are easy to maintain if you brush them daily. When they are puppies, brushing offers a fantastic way to bond.	$3.50 to $20
Toys	You definitely want to get toys for your puppy; you will want toys for more aggressive chewers, especially if your puppy goes through them quickly. Also, buy your adult Westie toys.	$2.00 Packs of toys range from $10 to $20 (which is easier in the long run as your pup will chew through toys quickly)
Training treats	You will need treats from the beginning and likely won't need to change the treats based on your Westie's age; you may need to change treats to keep your dog's interest, however.	$4.50 to $15

You will need to pay attention to when items need to be replaced based on your dog's size. Ultimately, you need to establish a budget for the initial costs, then create a second budget for items that will need to be replaced. Plan to revisit this list at the end of every year so you can make sure your dog remains comfortable and happy.

FUN FACT
A Shared Ancestor

West Highland White Terriers share a common ancestor with several other Terrier breeds that originated in Scotland. Scottie dogs, Dandie Dinmonts, Cairns, and Westies are all believed to have originated from the same type of dog. All of these dogs were bred for the same purpose: to hunt rodents and small game.

When you contact a vet to plan your first visit with your Westie, request an estimate for costs for that first year. The cost is substantially different for shots in a major city than in a rural area. Use the rough estimate for shots and other vet costs and add it to your budget planning for that first year—as well as getting that first vet visit on your calendar.

Instructing Your Children

In order to make your puppy feel comfortable in its new home, you must make sure your children are careful and gentle with the dog, whether you adopt a puppy or an adult dog. Since Westies look like living stuffed animals, some kids may try to treat the puppy like a toy, which could be detrimental to your dog. Take the time to make sure your children follow all of the "puppy rules" from the very beginning to ensure your puppy feels safe, happy, and isn't accidentally injured.

The following are the Five Golden Rules your children should follow from day one. They apply both to puppies and adult Westies:

(1) Always be gentle and respectful.

(2) Do not disturb the puppy during mealtime.

(3) Chase is an outside game.

(4) The Westie should always remain firmly on the ground. Never pick him up.

(5) All valuables should be kept out of the puppy's reach.

Since your kids are going to ask why these rules are necessary, the following are some explanations you can use. If necessary, modify the discussion to meet the audience—what you say to a toddler is a lot different than what you should tell a teen about playing with your Westie.

Always Be Gentle and Respectful

Little Westie puppies are ridiculously cute and cuddly, but they are also more fragile than adult dogs. At no time should anyone play roughly with a puppy. It is important to be respectful of your puppy to help him learn to also be respectful toward people and other animals.

This rule must be applied consistently every time your children play with your puppy. Be firm if you see your children getting too excited or rough. You don't want the puppy to get overly excited either because he might end up nipping or biting someone. If he does, it won't be his fault because he is still learning as a puppy. Make sure your children understand the possible repercussions if they get too rough.

Photo Courtesy of Terri Peterson

Mealtime

Westies can be protective of their food, especially if you rescue a dog that has previously had to fend for himself. Even if you have a puppy, you don't want him to feel insecure during his mealtime because he will learn to be aggressive whenever he eats. Save yourself, your family, and your dog from problems by making sure mealtime is your dog's time alone. Teach your children their own mealtime is off-limits to the puppy, as well.

No feeding your new dog from the table! From toddlers to teens, this is something you'll really need to emphasize—particularly for foods that your kids don't like. Westies are pets, not garbage disposals, and no amount of cute puppy eyes should be rewarded with scraps from the table. That is a recipe for disaster as it will get harder to convince your dog to stop begging if other people aren't following your rules.

Chase

Make sure your children understand why a game of chase is perfect for the outdoors (though you'll need to monitor things), but inside the house, chase is off limits!

Running inside your home gives your Westie puppy the impression your home isn't safe for him because he is being chased; it also teaches your puppy that running indoors is allowed, which can be dangerous as the dog gets older and bigger. One of the last things you want to see is your adult Westie (even if he isn't very big) go barreling through your home—knocking into people and furniture—because it was fine for him to run in the house when he was a puppy!

Paws on the Ground

It doesn't matter if your Westie looks like a stuffed animal—he is a living, breathing creature, and he needs to have his paws on the ground. Even though you might want to carry your new family member around or play with the pup like a baby, you and your family will have to resist that urge. The younger your children are, the more difficult it will be for them to understand the difference. It is so tempting to treat the puppy like a baby by carrying him around, but this is incredibly uncomfortable and unhealthy for the puppy.

Older children will quickly learn that a puppy's nip or bite hurts a lot more than one would think, and some Westies do nip. Those little teeth are quite sharp, and if he nips at you, he could accidentally be dropped—no one wants that to happen. If your children are never allowed to pick up the puppy, things will be a lot better for everyone involved. Remember, this also applies to you, so don't make things difficult by doing something you constantly tell your children not to do.

Keep Valuables Out of Reach

Your kids will be less than happy if their personal possessions are chewed up by an inquisitive puppy, so teach them to put toys, clothes, and other valuables far out of the puppy's reach.

Photo Courtesy
of Meghan Jackson

Preparing Your Current Dogs and Cats

Westies don't tend to be picky in the beginning. Puppies want to love everyone—people, dogs, and cats. To get the best dog possible, though, you should start socializing him with your other dogs or pets when he is still a puppy. In most cases, this is a fairly straightforward process as long as your pets are comfortable with you bringing a puppy into their home.

The following are important tasks you should complete when preparing your current pets for the new arrival:

- Set a schedule for activities and the people who will need to participate.
- Preserve your current dog's favorite places and furniture; make sure your current dog's toys and other personal items are not in the puppy's space.
- Have playdates at your home to observe your dog(s) reactions to having an addition to the house.

Stick to a Schedule

It's essential to have a schedule. Obviously, the puppy is going to receive a lot of attention in the beginning, so you need to make a concerted effort to be sure your current pets know you will still care for them. Set a specific time in your schedule when you can show your current dog(s) how much you love him (them), and make sure you don't stray from that schedule after the puppy arrives.

When you bring the puppy home, plan to have at least one adult present for each dog you have in your home. If you have a cat in the home, the introduction will need to be slow and methodical. If you bring home an adult Westie, you will need to be careful and keep the dog and cat separate when you aren't around to monitor them. Over time, it is likely they will learn to be fine with each other.

Having a schedule in place for your other dogs will make it easier to follow the plan with the puppy. Westies love to be prepared for what is about to happen—at least in the beginning.

Once he has arrived, your puppy is going to eat, sleep, and spend most of the day and night in his assigned space. This means your puppy's space cannot block your current canine's favorite furniture, bed, or anywhere he rests during the day. None of your current dog's "stuff" should be in the puppy's area either; this includes toys. You don't want your older dog to feel as if the puppy is taking over his territory. Make sure your children also understand to never put your current dog's things in the puppy's area!

Your dog and your puppy will need to be kept apart in the beginning (even if they seem friendly) until your puppy has received his vaccinations. Puppies are more susceptible to illness during these early days, so wait until the puppy is protected from possible diseases before the dogs spend time together. Leaving the puppy in his puppy space will keep them separated during this critical time.

Photo Courtesy
of Jolyn Zimmermann

Helping Your Dog Prepare – Extra at Home Playdates

The following explains strategies that will help prepare your current pooch for the arrival of your puppy:

- Consider the personality of your dog to predict what might happen when the puppy arrives. If your current dog loves other dogs, this will probably hold true when the puppy shows up. If your current dog is territorial, you will need to be cautious when introducing the two dogs, at least until the Westie has become part of the pack. Excitable dogs need special attention to keep from getting agitated when a new dog comes home. You don't want your current dog to be so excited that he makes the Westie feel threatened.

- Consider the times when unfamiliar dogs have been in your home. How did your current dog react to these other furry visitors? If your canine became territorial, be cautious when introducing your new pup. If you have never invited another dog into your home, organize a playdate with other dogs before your Westie puppy arrives. You need to know how your current furry babies will react to new dogs in the house so that you can properly prepare. Meeting a dog at home is quite different from encountering one outside the home.

- Think about your dog's interactions with other dogs for as long as you have known him. Has your dog shown protective or possessive behavior, either with you or others? Food is one of the reasons dogs will display aggression because they don't want anyone eating what is theirs. Some dogs can be protective of people and toys, too.

- If you know someone who owns a Westie, organize a playdate so that your current dog becomes aware of the temperament of a Westie.

These same rules apply, no matter how many dogs you have. Think about their individual personalities as well as how they interact together. Similar to humans, you may find when your dogs are together, they act differently. This is something you will need to keep in mind as you plan their first introduction. (Details of how to introduce your current dog(s) and your new puppy—plus how to juggle the two new personalities—are included in Chapter 8.)

CHAPTER 6

Preparing Your Home and Schedule

It doesn't matter whether you bring home a puppy or adult Westie; you are going to have your work cut out for you. It's almost exactly like child-proofing your home prior to the arrival of a baby or toddler. Adult Westies are not substantially larger than their puppy counterparts, so you will be taking many of the same steps to secure the different areas of your home, especially cabinets. Protecting your Westie is the priority, and this could be challenging if your Westie gets bored and decides to explore new places. You are going to spend a lot of time both inside and outside of your place, preparing it for your newest family member. That clever little Westie

Photo Courtesy of Georgia Mae Webster

Photo Courtesy
of Maxine Middleton

brain is going to start working out ways to get around barriers if you don't make sure to secure your new dog's designated area. Keep in mind, even an adult dog should be restricted in the beginning as he learns about your home and you learn more about his personality.

Even after you've completed the initial preparations, a weekly review leading up to your Westie's arrival is necessary to make sure you don't miss anything and that everything is in place. Your new family member should have a safe space that includes all of the essentials. This will help to ease your new pup's mind and make the initial arrival a great experience for everyone.

Westies do require proof that you are a leader they should follow, so you are going to need to earn your new family member's respect. This is why it is absolutely essential to ensure that you are firm and consistent when you are training and working with your Westie. When he understands that you mean what you say, that will go a long way to letting him know why he should listen to you.

Creating a Safe Space for Your Dog or Puppy

"Restrict their environment so learning can happen fast. Westies are very smart and will get into all kinds of trouble if left unsupervised. I have not found them to be chewers as much as some people, but they are definitely diggers, door openers, and food thieves."

MARLEEN C BURFORD
MARDOT

Your puppy will need a dedicated space that includes a crate, food and water bowls, pee pads, and toys. All of these things need to be in the area where the puppy will stay when you are not able to give him attention. The puppy's space should be gated so your Westie cannot get out and young children (or dogs) cannot get in. It should be a safe space where the puppy can see you going about your usual business and feel comfortable.

An adult Westie will need a similar setup as a puppy, with all of the same items, but you can give the adult dog a bigger area. Pee pads may be necessary while the adult dog adjusts to his new environment, even if he is already house trained.

HELPFUL TIP
Snuffle Mat

Westies were initially bred as small-game hunting dogs, and their prey instinct is stronger than most. This heightened prey drive can mean that Westies are harder on their toys and frequently enjoy burrowing. Purchasing a snuffle mat right away can give your Westie a positive and productive outlet for his habits. A snuffle mat is an interactive feeding toy, usually composed of a square of fabric with strips of cloth protruding from the top, that hides the food. You can feed whole meals on the mat to slow down overzealous eaters or hide a few treats in the fabric to entertain your pup.

Crates

Crate training can be fairly easy (covered in Chapter 7), but not if you have a crate that is too big, too small, or too uncomfortable for your dog to feel like it is a safe place. To make training easier, be sure the puppy's crate and bedding are set up and ready before your puppy arrives.

Never treat the crate like it is a prison for your puppy. It's meant to be a safe haven after overstimulation or when it's time to sleep. Ensure your dog never associates the crate with punishment or negative emotions. You can also get your puppy a carrying crate in the early days to make trips to the vet a little easier.

As mentioned in an earlier chapter, a crate can be used to help with house training. If you leave your Westie in his dedicated space, house training can be incredibly easy because dogs prefer to have a clean area. If the breeder has already started house training the puppy, this will make the job even easier.

Puppy-Proof/Dog-Proof the House

"A Westie puppy tends to be very curious, mischievous, and entertaining. Anything they can get into is considered 'fun' in their eyes. Puppy proofing your home is a must. A roll of toilet paper or paper towels can be an intriguing toy for your Westie, and you will find yourself walking into a 'snow storm' if one is kept within reach!"

MELANIE CLARK
Gap Kennels

The most dangerous rooms and items in your home will be as dangerous to your puppy as if he were a little baby. The biggest difference is your Westie is going to become mobile much faster than a child. He will get into dangerous situations immediately if you don't eliminate all the hazards before his arrival. Be aware that puppies will try to eat virtually anything! Nothing is safe—not even your furniture—and he will also gnaw on wood and metal. Anything within reach is considered fair game! Keep this in mind as you go about puppy-proofing your home. You will need to look for all of these dangers and make sure they are removed before your Westie arrives, whether he is a puppy or adult.

Plant Dangers

You will need to be mindful of the plants in and around your home that could be hazardous to your dog. The following are thirty-four kinds of plants that should not be within your dog's reach. Remember to check both inside and outside your home.

Mildly Toxic	Mildly to Moderately Toxic	Moderately Toxic	Moderately to Highly Toxic	Highly Toxic
Asparagus Fern	Aloe	Alocasia	Cactus	Brunfelsia
Begonia	Amaryllis	Arrowhead	Kalanchoe	Desert Rose
Ficus Benjamina	Calla Lily	Dieffenbachia		Flame Lily
Flamingo Flower	Cyclamen	Dracaena Fragrans		Kaffir Lily
Gardenia	Dracaena	English Ivy		Oleander
Geranium	Philodendron	Eucalyptus		Sago Palm
Golden Pothos		Peyote		Bird of Paradise (Strelitzia)
Jade Plant				
Schefflera				
Ti Plant				
ZZ Plant				

Indoor Hazards and Fixes

"All puppies chew, but Westies especially do! I've seen families bubble wrap furniture legs, or set them in coffee canisters to protect them from the puppy. Always make sure to keep them away from electrical cords or anything else that is harmful if chewed. Keep lots of chew toys on hand."

FRANCES ROBERSON
Nancy's Westies

A Westie will be an avid explorer, wanting to get into everything if given the opportunity, and anything that a child might be curious about, your Westie will likely want to explore, especially with his mouth. Get on your hands and knees and see each room from your Westie's perspective prior to his arrival—you will find at least one thing you missed previously.

Hazards	Fixes	Time Estimate
Kitchen		
Poisons	Keep in secure, child-proof cabinets or on high shelves.	30 min.
Trash Cans	Use a lockable trash can or keep it in a secure location.	10 min.
Appliances	Make sure all cords are out of reach.	15 min.
Human Food	Keep out of reach.	Constant (Start making it a habit!)
Floors		
Slippery Surfaces	Put down rugs or special mats designed to stick to the floor.	30 min. – 1 hour
Training Area	Train your Westie on non-slip surfaces.	Constant
Bathrooms		
Toilet Brush	Either have one that locks into the container or keep the brush out of reach.	5 min./bathroom
Poisons	Keep in secure, child-proof cabinets or on high shelves.	15 – 30 min./ bathroom
Toilets	Keep lids closed. Do not use automatic toilet-cleaning chemicals.	Constant (Start making it a habit!)
Cabinets	Keep locked with child-proof locks.	15 – 30 min./ bathroom
Laundry Room		
Clothing	Store clean and dirty clothes off the floor and out of reach.	15 – 30 min.
Poisons (bleach, pods/detergent, dryer sheets, and misc. poisons)	Keep in secure, child-proof cabinets or on high shelves.	15 min.

Hazards	Fixes	Time Estimate
Around the Home		
Plants	Keep off the floor.	45 min. – 1 hour
Trash Cans	Have a lockable trash can or keep it in a secure location.	10 – 30 min.
Electrical Cords/ Window Blind Cords	Hide cords or make sure they are out of reach; pay particular attention to entertainment and computer areas.	1 – 1.5 hours
Poisons	Check to make sure there aren't any in reach (WD40, window/screen cleaner, carpet cleaner, air fresheners); move all poisons to a central, locked location.	1 hour
Windows	Be sure cords are out of reach in all rooms.	1 – 2 hours
Fireplaces	Store cleaning supplies and tools where the puppy can't get into them. Cover the fireplace opening with something the puppy can't knock over.	10 min./fireplace
Stairs	Cordon off so that your puppy can't go up or down the stairs; make sure to test all puppy gates for safety.	10 – 15 min.
Coffee Tables/ End Tables/ Nightstands	Clear of dangerous objects (e.g., scissors, sewing equipment, pens, and pencils) and all valuables.	30 – 45 min.

If you have a cat, keep the litter box off the floor. It needs to be somewhere that your cat can easily get to it, but your Westie cannot. Since this involves training your cat, it's something you should do well in advance of the puppy's arrival. You don't want your cat to undergo too many significant changes all at once. The new canine in the house will be enough of a disruption! If your cat associates the change with your Westie, you may find the feline refusing to use the litter box.

To get the litter box out of your dog's reach, you'll need to put it up high and preferably somewhere that doesn't have a chair that your dog can use. Clever pups can figure out how to get to places where you think they shouldn't be able to go.

Finally, in case of problems, be sure your vet's number is posted on the fridge and in at least one other room in the house. Even if the number is programmed into your phone, family members or dog-sitters will still need to know who to call.

Photo Courtesy of Carolyn Friedman

Outdoor Hazards and Fixes

The area outside your home also needs dog-proofing. As with the inside, you will need to check your outdoor preparations by getting down low and inspecting all areas from a puppy's perspective. Again, you are all but guaranteed to find at least one thing you missed. Remember to also post the vet's number in one of the sheltered outdoor areas in case of an emergency.

Hazards	Fixes	Time Estimate
Garage		
Poisons	Keep in secure, child-proof cabinets or on high shelves (e.g., car chemicals, cleaning supplies, paint, lawn care) – this includes fertilizer.	1 hour
Trash Bins	Keep them in a secure location.	5 min.
Tools (e.g., lawn, car, hardware, power tools)	Make sure all cords are kept out of reach and never hang over the side of surfaces.	30 min. – 1 hour
Equipment (e.g., sports, fishing)	Keep out of reach and never allow them to hang over the side of surfaces.	Constant (Start making it a habit!)
Sharp Implements	Keep out of reach and never allow them to hang over the side of surfaces.	30 min.
Bikes	Store off the ground or in a place the Westie cannot get to (to keep the pup from biting the tires).	20 min.
Fencing (Can Be Done Concurrently)		
Breaks	Fix any breaks in the fencing. You need to make sure your Westie can't easily get out of your yard.	30 min. – 1 hour

Hazards	Fixes	Time Estimate
Gaps	Fill any gaps, even if they are intentional, so your Westie doesn't escape.	30 min. – 1 hour
Holes/Dips at Base	Fill any area that can be easily crawled under.	1 – 2 hours
Yard		
Poisons	Don't leave any poisons in the yard.	1 – 2 hours
Plants	Verify that low plants aren't poisonous; fence off anything that is (such as grapevines).	45 min. – 1 hour

If you have a pool, make sure it is secure so that your dog cannot get into it without your help. Covers may not always be enough (especially for intelligent breeds that may want to swim on their own terms), so make sure to have fencing or some other kind of deterrent to keep your Westie safe. Even if your dog loves swimming, make sure you are always around when your dog is in the pool—especially if it is an accidental swim. Westies can swim, but usually not for long, so make sure that they are protected.

Never leave your Westie alone in the garage, even when he is an adult. Your puppy may be in the garage when you take car trips, which is why it is important to puppy-proof this area.

Schedule fence inspections at least once a month after bringing home your new dog. Westies are proficient diggers, which means you are going to need to see if your pup has managed to create holes. This is also why you can never leave your Westie alone outside. You will always need to attend to your dog when he goes out to the bathroom or to play because when he is bored, he will very likely start to dig. You don't want to put him out to use the bathroom only to find he has escaped in the five minutes you left him outside alone.

It's helpful to have a dedicated digging space for your dog. We'll go into that a bit later, but for now, be aware of how much time you are going to need to dedicate to ensuring your Westie can't easily get out through holes or gaps in your fencing.

Choosing Your Veterinarian

You should choose a vet before you bring your dog home because scheduling a veterinary appointment may take a while. Fortunately, with a breed like the Westie, you'll probably find vets who have experience with the breed. It isn't likely that they'll have specialized in the breed, but they should have a good idea of how best to tend to your dog during appointments.

Photo Courtesy of Roy Poh

Every dog, regardless of age, should see a vet within the first forty-eight hours of his arrival home. The point is to establish your dog's baseline health. This may also be a requirement included in the contract with the breeder. Twenty-four hours is strongly recommended to make sure your dog is healthy, but this may not always be possible, which is why many places say to have it done within 48 hours. If there is a vet near you who specializes in or has worked with Westies before, that will be best for your pup.

The following are some things to consider when looking for a vet:

- What is the vet's level of familiarity with Westies?

The vet doesn't have to be a specialist, but a vet with experience with the breed is helpful. As popular and long-lived as the Westie breed is, you can ask if the vet has treated Westies before. Even if the vet has only worked with one Westie before, it is beneficial since he can help explain what to expect in the different stages of your dog's life.

- How far from your home is the vet?

You don't want the vet to be more than thirty minutes away in case of an emergency.

- Is the vet available for emergencies after hours, or can they recommend a vet in case of an emergency?
- Is the vet part of a local veterinary hospital, or does the vet refer patients to a local pet hospital?
- Is the vet one of several partners, or does he work alone? If he or she belongs to a partnership, can your dog see the same vet for all office visits?
- How are appointments booked?
- Can other services be performed at the clinic, such as grooming and boarding?
- Is the vet accredited?
- What is the price for the initial visit? What are the prevailing costs for routine visits that might include such things as shots?
- What tests and checks are performed during the initial visit?
- Can you visit the vet you are considering before you bring your dog home?

If so, inspect the office environment and ask if you can speak to the vet. He or she should be willing to put you at ease and to answer your questions. Even though a vet's time is valuable, he should take a few minutes to help you feel confident about your decision to trust him with your new dog's health.

CHAPTER 7
Bringing Your West Highland White Terrier Home

"The best advice for bringing a new Westie into your home is making sure it's escape proof. Providing a secure environment, including a crate, bed and a few toys will go a long way in making your new family member comfortable. Another wonderful tip is not to overwhelm your new family member. Give them time to sniff through your home. Young children need to give a Westie room to become secure in their new environment."

CHRISTOPHER LARSON
West Highland White Terrier

*Photo Courtesy
of Betsy Davison*

When your Westie arrives home for the first time, it is going to be a memory that lasts for years. Laughs are nearly guaranteed as your new family member begins a hesitant—or overly enthusiastic—exploration of the new place. Regardless of his level of curiosity, your Westie is going to be anxious because he doesn't know any of you.

Even though Westies are known for being gregarious and adventurous, new experiences may be a bit overwhelming or scary for any dog. You'll need to take the time to make things comfortable and safe for your new Westie and your family. Go slow in the beginning as you introduce and socialize your new dog with other family members and pets so that your new addition isn't too overwhelmed.

This chapter covers how to introduce your new Westie to your home. If you already have a dog, refer to Chapter 8 because you will need to introduce the animals outside of the home before your pup makes that grand entrance. Once you understand how to introduce dogs to each other, come back here to see how to introduce your new family member to your home and any family members who weren't able to make the initial meet and greet.

Final Preparations and Planning

Your new pup is likely to have separation anxiety, and there is a lot you can do to prepare for that, starting with taking time from work during the first twenty-four to forty-eight hours; the best-case scenario would have you at home for the first week or two. The more time you dedicate to helping your new little friend become accustomed to his surroundings, the better.

Ensure You Have Food and Other Supplies on Hand

The day before your Westie arrives, review the list you created in Chapter 5 and do a quick check to ensure you have everything you need. Take a few moments to consider if there is anything you are missing. This will save you from having to rush out for additional supplies after the arrival of your new family member.

Design a Tentative Puppy Schedule

Prepare a tentative schedule to help you get started over the course of the first week. Your days are about to get remarkably busy, so you need somewhere to begin before your puppy arrives.

The following are three key areas to establish before your puppy arrives:

- Feeding
- Training (including house training)
- Playing

When you bring home a puppy, you may be expecting a ball of high energy. However, puppies of any breed (no matter how active they will be later) sleep between 18 and 20 hours per day. Having a predictable sleep schedule will help your puppy grow up healthier.

In the beginning, you won't need to worry about making sure that your puppy is tired out by the end of the day. His stamina will build fairly quickly, though; by the end of the first year, your pup will be a lot more active! As your pup starts to sleep less and play more, he will need 30 to 60 minutes of daily physical activity. In the early days, though, your puppy's schedule will revolve around sleeping and eating—with some walking and socialization. Waking hours will include training and play.

Do a Quick Final Puppy-Readiness Inspection Before the Puppy Arrives

No matter how busy you are or how carefully you follow the puppy-proofing checklist, the day before your puppy arrives, be sure to set aside an hour or two to double-check that everything is in place.

Initial Meeting

Review the rules in Chapter 5 with all family members the day of the dog's arrival and before the pup actually arrives. Place heavy emphasis on how to handle the Westie, particularly the part about not picking up your newest family member. The puppy is already going to be in a state of shock, so don't compound that by literally taking the world out from under your Westie's feet.

Determine who is going to be responsible for primary puppy care and for primary training. To teach younger children responsibility, a parent can pair with a child to manage the puppy's care. The child can be responsible for feeding the puppy and keeping the water bowl filled. Of course, a parent should oversee these tasks.

Picking up Your Puppy or Dog and the Ride Home

A good bit of planning and preparation goes into picking up your puppy, especially if you are going to the breeder's home. If possible, do this on a weekend or during a holiday weekend or season. This will allow you unrushed, quality time at home with your new puppy.

As tempting as it is to cuddle the puppy in your lap, it is both safer and more comfortable for the puppy if you use a crate for the ride home; two adults should also be present for the ride. This is the time to start teaching your puppy that car trips are enjoyable. This means making sure that the crate is securely anchored; you don't want the crate to slide around while he is helplessly sitting inside. This would be a terrifying experience for the puppy!

- The crate should be anchored in the car for safety and should include a cushion. If you have a long trip, bring food and water for the puppy and plan to stop at different intervals. Do not put food and water in the crate; sloshing water can scare your puppy. You can cover the bottom of the crate with a towel or pee pad in case of accidents.

- Call the breeder to make sure everything is still on schedule.

- Arrange for the mother dog to leave her scent on a blanket to help make the puppy's transition more comfortable.

- Make sure the second adult will be on time so that the two of you can head to the pick-up destination.

- If you have other dogs, make sure all of the adults involved in the introduction process know what to do. They should know the time and place for that first neutral territory meeting.

Photo Courtesy
of Cheryl Kellar

If you do not have other dogs, you can pick up your puppy and head straight home. If you have a trip that lasts more than a couple of hours, stop periodically so your puppy can stretch, exercise, drink, and use the bathroom. Keep your puppy away from other dogs until he has gotten all of his shots; you don't want him to be exposed to a dog that is carrying a disease that your puppy is not fully protected against.

At no point should your puppy be left alone in the car. If you have to use the restroom, either go before leaving the breeder, or if you have a longer drive ahead of you, have at least one adult remain with the puppy during each stop.

If the puppy has never ridden in a car before, a second person should show the puppy attention while the other person drives. The puppy will be in the crate, but someone can still provide comfort. The puppy will definitely be scared without his mom, siblings, or familiar people to console him. Having an adult present to talk to the puppy will make it less of an ordeal for the little guy.

When you arrive home, immediately take the puppy outside to use the bathroom. Even if he had an accident in his crate, this is the time to start training your new family member where to use the bathroom.

The First Vet Visit and What to Expect

The first vet visit will establish a baseline for the puppy's health. This will also allow the vet to track your puppy's progress and monitor his health as he grows. In addition to providing a chance to ask questions and get advice, this initial assessment will give you more information about your puppy. It also creates an important rapport between your Westie and the vet.

During that first veterinary visit, your pup won't know what to expect. Try to ease his anxiety; you want this first appointment to set a positive tone for all future visits. This will likely be trickier with an adult dog than with a puppy, so be prepared to soothe any nervousness. As friendly as the breed tends to be, this is still a lot of changes in a very short period of time.

The following is a list of several things that must be completed before the day of the appointment:

- Find out how early you need to arrive to complete the paperwork for the new patient.
- Find out if you should bring a stool sample for that first visit. If so, collect it the morning of the visit and make sure to take it with you.

FUN FACT
Celebrity dogs

Westies are a celebrity favorite, with famous owners such as Whoopi Goldberg, Scarlett Johansson, and Matthew McConaughey. Actor Robert Pattinson of Twilight fame grew up with a Westie named Patty, who he once described as being like his sister. Friends star Jennifer Aniston also owned a Westie and Corgi mix named Norman, who passed away at the age of 15.

- Bring the paperwork provided by the breeder or rescue organization for the vet to add to your dog's records.

Upon your arrival, your Westie may want to meet the other pups and people in the office and will probably announce your arrival. Although you will need to be mindful, this is an opportunity to socialize the puppy and to create a positive experience with the vet. Before letting your puppy meet other animals, always ask the owner for permission and wait for approval. Most pets at the vet's office are likely to not be feeling well, which means they may not be very affable. You don't want a grumpy, older dog or a sick animal to nip or scare your puppy. Negative social experiences are situations your puppy will remember; they could make future visits to the vet something to dread. Nor do you want your puppy to be exposed to potential illnesses before he has had all his shots.

Every vet is different, so you should call your vet ahead of that first visit to get an idea of everything that will be done. Odds are, you will need to bring documentation about your dog, so this can also serve as a reminder to get your paperwork together and ready to go with you and your newest family member when you go to the vet the first time. Anything that has not been documented that your vet feels is necessary (such as shots) will likely be done during that first visit. The dog's age will also affect what the vet does, though usually not by much. Young puppies will need a series of shots, and your vet is going to talk about that with you, but this isn't really a concern for an older dog. They may also request that you bring your dog's latest poop to check it for parasites. As gross as this may be, it is better to show up with that on the first visit so that you can get your new dog a clean bill of health or start treatments. Chapter 16 provides more details on what to expect if parasites are detected in your dog's bowel movement.

Be prepared for the vet to ask about your dog's history, even though you just brought the Westie home with you. Often people have more details about the dog than documentation because you probably talked with the breeder or rescuers to see what they know about your dog's history.

During the first visit, the vet will conduct an initial assessment of your Westie. One of the most important things the vet will do is weigh your dog. This is something you are going to have to monitor for your dog's entire life as you will want to ensure that your Westie remains at a healthy weight. Keep a record of his weight so you can see how quickly your puppy is growing and to make sure you aren't overfeeding your dog. Ask your vet what is considered a healthy weight for every growth stage and record that as well. Your Westie puppy will be adult-sized by the end of the first year, so make sure your new pup reaches that size in a healthy amount of time—not gaining excessive weight over just a few months.

The vet will set a date for the next group of shots, which will likely happen not too long after the initial visit. After your Westie receives his vaccinations (detailed in Chapter 16), prepare for a couple of days of your puppy feeling under the weather.

While both of these are important, the following are other checks the vet may make during that initial visit.

- Most vets will listen to your dog's heart and lungs to make sure there aren't any obvious problems.
- They will take your pup's temperature, so be prepared to help by calming your dog as he's probably not going to be happy with this activity.
- Vets usually check a dog's ears, eyes, nose, paws, skin/coat, and genitals.
- They will do a longer check on the mouth and teeth to look for potential problems.
- They will do an initial check on the abdomen and lymph nodes.

If the vet does find a problem and recommends medication, take the time to ask questions and make sure you know what to do before you leave the office.

Crate and Other Preliminary Training

"I recommend putting your new Westie puppies crate in a private room (like an extra bathroom or laundry room) when it's time for bed. Westies usually will not 'wind down' on their own. A private room will let the puppy settle down peacefully, otherwise any movement or sound will keep them distracted and it will take them longer to settle down. They do get bored easily, so always have a dog bone in their crate to keep them busy."

LEA LESLIE
Westiesworldforever

Contrary to what some people think, crates are a safe space for dogs. It is kind of like their own room. Even Westies may want a little time on their own, and that is what their crate provides. For you, the crate is a place where your Westie can stay safe, especially if he has separation anxiety. Your stuff and your dog are protected from any destructive tendencies. Crate training will prepare your dog for occasions when you may have to board him, and he will be put in a crate if you ever travel on a plane.

✓ Puppies younger than six months should not be left in a crate for hours at a time. Your Westie will not be able to hold his bladder for very long, so you must make sure he has a way to get out and to go to the bathroom. If you adopt an adult Westie that is not house trained, you will need to follow the same rules. If you aren't sure about whether or not the dog is house trained, it is best to treat the adult like a puppy until you are certain that your newest family member won't use the house as a bathroom.

Make sure the crate door is set so that it doesn't close on your dog during his initial sniff of the crate. You do not want your Westie to be scared by the door as it is closing behind him; this could make him fearful of the crate in the future.

The following are some suggestions:

- Use a positive, cheerful voice as you let your Westie sniff the crate for the first time. The first experience in the crate should be associated with excitement and positive emotions. Be sure your dog understands the crate is a good place. If you have a blanket from the puppy's mother, put it in the crate to help provide an extra sense of comfort.

- Drop a couple of treats into the crate if your canine seems reluctant to enter. Do NOT force your dog into the crate. If your dog refuses to go all the way inside the crate, that is perfectly fine. It has to be HIS decision to enter, so it doesn't become a negative experience.

- For a week or two, feed your dog while he is in the crate. Besides keeping the food away from any other pets, this will create positive associations between your Westie and the crate.
    - If your dog appears comfortable with the crate, put the food all the way at the back.
    - If not, place the food bowl in the front, then move it further back in the crate over time.

- Start closing the door once your dog appears to be eating comfortably in the crate. When the food is gone, open the crate door immediately.

- Leave the door closed for longer periods of time after your dog has finished eating. If your pup begins to whine, you know you have left your Westie in the crate for too long.

- Crate your dog for longer periods of time once he shows no signs of discomfort in the crate when he is eating. Train him to go into the crate by simply saying, "Crate" or "Bed." Then, praise your dog and let him know that he has done an excellent job.

Repeat these steps for several weeks until your dog seems comfortable in his crate. The regular repetition several times a day teaches your dog that the crate is not a punishment and everything is alright. Initially, you should do this while you are still at home or when you go out to get the mail. When you leave the room and your puppy lasts half an hour without whining, you can leave the dog alone for longer periods of time. However, keep this alone time to no more than an hour in the beginning.

During the first few weeks, you should also begin to house train your Westie. Basic behavioral training is also vital from the start. However, wait until your Westie has all of his vaccinations before taking your new puppy to structured training classes. Knowledgeable trainers will not accept puppies in their classes until a dog's first full round of shots is complete.

Chapter 12 provides a closer look at how to train your dog.

First Night Frights

"Your Westie puppy will probably cry the first few nights. Put him in a crate correctly sized for him with a blanket and/or a soft toy. Keep the crate next to your bed so that he will be soothed by your presence. Sometimes covering the crate with a towel or blanket will help to make him feel more secure."

NORA BALIN STONE
Balinbrae Westies

That first night is going to be terrifying for your little Westie puppy! As understandable as this may be, there is only so much comfort you can give your new family member. The more you respond to his cries and whimpering, the more he will learn negative behavior provides the desired results. You need to prepare for a balancing act—one that reassures the Westie that he is safe while keeping him from associating crying with receiving attention from you.

Create a sleeping area for your puppy near where you sleep. The area should have the puppy's bed tucked safely into his crate. This will offer him a safe place to hide and a place where he will feel more comfortable in this strange new home. The entire area should be blocked off to be sure no one can get in (and the puppy can't get out) during the night. This sleeping area

Photo Courtesy of Letty Zemaitis

should also be close to where people sleep so that the puppy doesn't feel abandoned. If you were able to get a blanket or pillow that smells like the mother, make sure that this is in your puppy's space. Consider adding a little white noise (like an old-fashioned alarm clock) to cover unfamiliar sounds that could scare your new pet.

Your puppy will make noises over the course of the night. Don't move the puppy away, even if the whimpering keeps you awake. Being moved away from people will only scare the puppy more, reinforcing the anxiety he feels. When your puppy whines during the night, he is not whimpering because he's been in the crate too long. He's scared or wants someone to be with him—he's probably never been alone at night before coming to live with you. Spare yourself trouble later on by teaching the puppy that whimpering will not get him out of the crate. Over time, being close to you at night will be enough to reassure your puppy that everything will be fine.

In the beginning, puppies will need to go to the bathroom every two to three hours. This means you will also need to get up during the night! Make sure your puppy understands he must always go to the bathroom outside before bedtime or on the pee pad. If you ignore this rule, you will have a tough time training him to only relieve himself outside and not in the house.

If you choose to let your dog on the bed, wait until he is house trained. Otherwise, you might have to replace your mattress within a short time. It is best to simply keep your Westie off the furniture so that he doesn't get hurt and your furniture doesn't get ruined!

CHAPTER 8
Introducing Your Westie to Your Other Dogs

"Westies are social by nature, so if you put them in a safe space with an-other friendly dog, it will likely happen naturally. Make sure you research your breeder and choose one who socializes pups (with humans and other pups) from an early age. It's essential to have that socially healthy beginning!"

FRANCES ROBERSON

Nancy's Westies

Westies are typically easy dogs to introduce into the home, but adults could be a challenge, depending on how much they were socialized when they were puppies. Nearly all dogs are hesitant initially when they meet another dog in a completely new environment, but Westies are a breed that tends to warm up quickly to everyone. The younger a dog is when you start socialization, the more quickly he will feel comfortable with other dogs and pets.

FUN FACT

Best In Show

A West Highland White Terrier first won the annual Westminster Kennel Club Dog Show Best in Show title in 1942. This dog's name was Ch. Wolvey Pattern of Edgerstoune and was owned by Mrs. J. G. Winant. A Westie won this title again in 1962. As of 2021, a Westie has won this title only twice.

It is actually best if you have at least one other dog so that your Westie isn't home alone while you are out shopping or at work. If you already have a socialized adult dog, your current dog can also help teach your new Westie the rules, and he could even become a mentor to your puppy. When your Westie sees your dog listening to your commands, he will imitate this behavior, something that could be really helpful with a potentially stubborn breed. However, this works both ways. If your current dog displays negative behavior, you should try to correct these habits before your puppy arrives. You don't want your Westie pup learning bad habits.

Introducing Your New Puppy to Your Other Pets

Introduce all new dogs to your current dog or dogs, regardless of age, in a neutral place away from your home. Even if you have never had problems with your current dog, you are about to change his world. When introducing your dog to the new puppy, select a park or other public area so your current dog will not feel territorial. This gives both animals the opportunity to meet and become familiar with each other on neutral ground.

When introducing the two dogs, make sure you have at least one other adult with you so that there's one person for each canine. All dogs should be leashed so that you can quickly and easily move them apart if the introduction does not go well. If you have more than two dogs, then you should have one adult per dog. This will make it easier to keep all of the dogs under control. Even the best dogs can get excited about meeting a puppy. One of the people who needs to be at this meeting is the person who is in charge of the pets in your home. This helps establish the pack hierarchy.

Don't hold your puppy in your arms when the dogs meet. While you may want to protect the puppy, holding him has the opposite effect. Instead, your puppy will feel trapped, but if the puppy is on the ground, he can run if he feels scared. Stand near the puppy with your feet a little bit apart, so he can hide behind your legs if he decides he needs to escape.

All dogs should have a few minutes to sniff each other, making sure there is always some slack in each leash. Feeling like they can move more freely helps dogs to relax, and they won't feel like you are trying to restrain them or force them into something. Your dog will either want to play, or he might simply ignore the puppy. You need to let your dog dictate what happens next. If the dogs want to play, be careful your current dog doesn't accidentally hurt the puppy, and if your dog ends up ignoring the puppy after an initial sniff, that is fine too. If your dog is clearly unhappy, keep all of the dogs apart until everyone is comfortable with the meeting. Don't force the situation.

This introduction could take a while, depending on each individual dog's personality. The friendlier and more accepting your current dog is, the easier it will be to incorporate your new puppy into the home, especially for dogs like Westies that love being around others. For some dogs, a week is enough time to start feeling comfortable together. For other dogs, it could take a couple of months before they are fully accepting of a new puppy. Since this is a completely new dynamic for your dog, he may be angry with you for bringing this new bundle of energy into his life.

The older your current dog is, the more likely it is that a puppy will be an unwelcome addition. Older dogs can get cranky around a puppy that doesn't know when enough is enough! The goals are to make your puppy feel welcome and safe and to let your older dog know that your love for him is as strong as ever.

Once your new family member and the rest of the canine pack become acquainted and comfortable, you can head home. When you arrive, take the dogs into the yard and remove the leashes. Again, you will need one adult per dog, including the puppy. If the dogs are all right or are indifferent to the puppy, you can let your current dog inside. Then, re-leash the puppy, keeping him on the leash as you go inside.

Put the puppy in the puppy area when the introductions are complete. Remember to make sure your current dog cannot get into this area and your puppy cannot get out.

Introducing an Adult Dog to Other Pets

Always approach the introduction (and first few weeks together) with caution. The new adult Westie will need his own things from the very beginning—Westies can be territorial if not properly trained. When you aren't around, your dog should be kept in a separate area so there won't be any fighting among the dogs.

Plan for this introduction to take at least an hour. Since the dogs are both adults, they will need to move and become acquainted at their own pace.

When introducing your current dog(s) to your new dog, follow the same steps as you would with a puppy:

- Begin in neutral territory.

- Ask one adult to be present for each adult canine during the introduction.

- Introduce one dog at a time. Don't let several dogs meet your new Westie all at once.

Bring treats to the meeting of two adult dogs—unlike with puppies. The animals will respond to the treats, and if the atmosphere becomes tense, the treats will create a distraction.

During the introduction, watch the Westie and your dog(s) to see if any of them raises his hackles. This is one of the first obvious signs that a dog is uncomfortable. If the Westie's hackles are up, back off the introductions for a little bit. Do this by calling your current dog back first. This is also when you should start waving treats around! Avoid pulling on the leashes to separate the dogs. You don't want to add physical tension to the situation because that could trigger a fight. Treats will work for all dogs, and calling their names should help get things under control.

If any of the dogs are showing their teeth or growling, call your dog back and give the dogs a chance to settle down. Use treats and a calming voice to get them to relax. You want all the dogs to feel comfortable during the first meeting, so don't force the friendship. If they seem uncomfortable or wary at first, let them move at their own pace.

Older Dogs and Your West Highland White Terrier

If your current dog is older, keep in mind puppies are energetic, and they want to engage older dogs in their play. This can be very trying for your older canine, so make sure your older dog doesn't get too tired of the puppy's antics. A tired, older dog could snap and nip at your puppy in hopes of getting a little rest. You don't want your puppy to begin snapping at other dogs too. Watch for signs your older dog is ready for some alone time, some time with you, or simply a break from the puppy.

You should always make sure your older dog has safe places where he can be alone. This is essential for those times he just doesn't feel up to being around a spry, young puppy! By keeping your puppy and your older dog separate, you can prevent the need for constant scolding. Plus, the puppy will not become wary of older dogs.

Even if you own an adult Westie, he might be too energetic for your older dog to handle. Westies may be active dogs at any age! Be mindful and make sure your dog's golden years are not marred by a new canine that wants to play in a way your older dog can't. Westies are more likely to understand limits and boundaries faster than many other breeds, but you want to minimize how annoyed your older dog is while your puppy is learning those boundaries.

Dog Aggression and Territorial Behavior

Westies are incredibly affectionate and happy with dogs and cats they know, but there may be a level of dominance or aggression toward dogs they don't know. This is one of the primary reasons why you should never let your Westie off-leash. (Details on how to train your Westie are discussed in Chapter 12.)

There are two types of aggression you should watch for:

- Dominance aggression is when your dog wants to show control over another animal or person. This kind of aggression can be seen in the following behaviors and in reaction to anyone going near the Westie's belongings (like toys or a food bowl):
    - Growling
    - Nipping
    - Snapping

This is the behavior that the pack leader uses to warn others not to touch his stuff. If you see this reaction in your Westie while he is around you, a family member, or another pet, you must intervene immediately. Correct him by saying, "No," then lavish him with praise when he stops. You must consistently intervene whenever your Westie behaves in this manner.

Do not leave your Westie alone with other people, dogs, or animals as long as any dominance aggression is exhibited. If you are not there to

intervene, your dog will push boundaries and will likely try to show his dominance over those around him. Never train your Westie to react aggressively!

Once you are sure this behavior has been eliminated, you can leave your current dog and Westie alone for short periods of time. You should remain in another room or somewhere in close proximity but out of sight. Over time, you can leave your pets alone when you get the mail; then, try leaving them when you run errands or longer tasks. Eventually, you will be able to leave your Westie alone with other dogs without worrying that he will show dominance to others.

Feeding Time Practices

Your Westie puppy will be fed in his puppy space, so mealtime will not be a problem in the beginning.

The following are suggestions for feeding your puppy when he is around the other dogs; this will reduce the chance of territorial behavior:

- Feed your Westie at the same time as the other dogs but in a different room. Keeping them separated will let your Westie eat without distractions or feeling that your other dogs will eat what is in his bowl. Make sure to feed your Westie in the same room each time while the other dogs eat in their established areas.

- Keep your Westie and other dogs in their areas until they finish eating their food. Some dogs have a tendency to leave food in the bowl. Don't let them. They need to finish everything because all food bowls will be removed as soon as the dogs finish eating.

- Make sure you have someone near your Westie so that he learns not to growl at people near his bowl. This will help reduce stress when other dogs are around the food. If your dog demonstrates any aggression, immediately correct him by saying, "No," then give him praise when he stops. Do not play with the food bowl, and make sure none of the kids play with it. Your dog needs to know that no one is going to try to steal his food.

- Over the course of a couple of weeks, move your dogs closer together while eating. For example, you can feed your current dog on one side of the door near the doorway and the Westie on the opposite side.

- After a month or two, you can feed the dogs in the same room but with some distance between them. If your Westie starts to exhibit protective behavior with the other dogs, correct him, then praise him when he stops the behavior.

Photo Courtesy
of Abigail Orenstein

Eventually, you can start feeding the dogs close to one another. This can take weeks to months to accomplish, depending on the age of the Westie. A puppy will need less time because he will be socialized with the dogs from an early age, making him less wary. That does not mean he won't display territorial behavior. Yet, it likely won't take long for him to start to feel comfortable eating near the rest of the pack.

For adult dogs, this process could take longer, and you should not rush it. Let your dog learn to feel comfortable eating before you make changes, even small ones. Dogs of any breed can be protective of their food, depending on their past history. Before your dog will eat peacefully, he must be assured that his protective behavior is not necessary around other dogs. That means letting his confidence and his comfort level build at his own pace.

CHAPTER 9
The First Few Weeks

Westies really don't have a ramping-up period—pretty much as soon as you get home, your pup is likely to want to start exploring. Be prepared for two speeds—energetic and sleeping. It isn't likely that there will be much in between because this is a dog that is used to being on the go. Coupled with their intelligence, Westies are curious and enthusiastic nearly as soon as they can walk. When your dog is not sleeping, you may find yourself feeling that you can't get a moment's rest—but in a fun and entertaining way. The bond you and your Westie form in those early days will be important in establishing the relationship you have over the years.

By the end of the first month, your pup should be sleeping through the night. As Westies prefer a clean surrounding, house training can be very easy and probably won't take as long before your puppy knows where to go to the bathroom. Having a great breeder who starts the process will further speed up how quickly he learns. You will want to monitor your Westie, though, and never let a puppy or dog out of his dedicated area alone during that first week.

The first month is when you really need to start paying attention to your puppy's emerging personality. As with all intelligent breeds, the key is to remain consistent when it comes to training. That means everyone should be consistent, including the kids. Always use what you learn about your puppy's personality to encourage good behavior!

HELPFUL TIP
Nighttime Waking

Puppies have smaller bladder capacities than older dogs and will need to wake multiple times during the night for the first few weeks to avoid soiling the house. A good rule of thumb is that dogs can hold their bladder for as many hours as their age in months plus one. Some new puppy owners may be tempted to keep their puppy in bed with them to avoid being woken by crying at night, but because of your Westie's size, he is much safer in a crate in your bedroom or another safe place until fully grown. A puppy falling from bed can cause severe injury and even death.

Setting the Rules and Sticking to Them

"Start off with a schedule, and stick with it. Westies love structure (and need it), and they adjust better if you stick to the program from the very beginning."

MELANIE CLARK
Gap Kennels

This goes for both your dog and your kids, regardless of the age of the dog or kid. You don't want your older children or teens undoing your hard work by letting the new Westie out to roam. Given the dog's size, this is a dog that can plan for when to go to the bathroom without being caught by anyone else. Make sure everyone knows that the rules apply to everyone. This will be better for your kids and your new pup.

Your puppy needs to understand the rules and to know you and your family mean them, even if the dog really doesn't like what you are saying. Once your canine learns to follow your commands, there will still be times when he will refuse to obey. That is nearly a certainty. However, he will be much more likely to listen when he knows you are in control.

Establish a No Jumping and No Mouthing Policy

"Be prepared to teach your Westie what they can chew, and can't chew. If they chew on something they should not be chewing on, it is important to remove it and immediately give them something they already love to chew up."

LEA LESLIE
Westiesworldforever

If not properly trained, a Westie may jump on you in greeting, and this can be very bad if the dog tries to jump on little children. Such a sturdy build can easily knock over a toddler without meaning to do it. You have the responsibility to ensure that your dog and children learn how to play properly. For your Westie, this means no jumping on people. Any games that involve biting or nipping should always be avoided. You do not want your Westie to ever think that nipping is all right. This will be very difficult if you don't enforce the rule right from the beginning.

Nipping

Westies (or any dog) are likely to nip under two conditions. Most situations where dogs nip are related to these two scenarios.

- One of the triggers for nipping is overstimulation. This can be one sign your puppy is too tired to keep playing or training, and you should put him to bed.
- Another trigger could be that your canine has too much energy. If this is the case, take your puppy outside to burn off some of his excess energy. At the same time, be careful not to over-exercise the puppy.

You need to be vigilant and immediately let your puppy know nipping is not acceptable. Some people recommend using a water spritzer bottle and spraying the puppy while saying, "No," after nipping. This is one of the few times when punishment may be effective, and it is probably essential. Remember— make sure your dog does not associate the spraying with anything other than his nipping. He needs to understand that he is getting sprayed because he is nipping someone and that this is not acceptable behavior.

Always firmly tell your puppy, "No," whenever he is nipping, even if it is during playtime. You should also pull away and loudly say, "Ouch!" to let your puppy know his teeth are hurting you. This will help to establish the idea that nipping is bad and is never rewarded.

81

*Photo Courtesy
of Karlee Steen*

Chewing

All puppies chew to relieve the pain of teething. Whether your dog is chewing on your furniture, utensils, or clothing, be sure to discourage this behavior as quickly as possible:

- Make sure you have toys for your Westie (whether an adult or a puppy) so that you can teach him what objects are acceptable for chewing. Having a lot of available toys and rotating those toys out will give your puppy or dog several options.

- If your puppy is teething, either refrigerate a couple of toys so that they are cold or give your puppy frozen carrots. The cold will help to numb the pain. Teething usually starts at between three and four months old, and it usually ends by eight months. You want to get toys that will be safe for his teeth in case your Westie has problems. Chapter 13 also provides details on diets that may help dogs with allergies, such as a raw diet.

- Toys that are made either of hard rubber or hard nylon are best, particularly Kongs with kibble in them. You can even fill them with water and freeze them, which will give your puppy something cool to soothe the pain of teething.

For the most part, keeping an eye on your dog when he is not in his designated space will help you quickly see when he is chewing on things he shouldn't. When this happens, firmly say, "No." If your dog continues to chew, put him back in his space. While he is in the space, make sure he has plenty of toys to chew on.

If you decide to use chew deterrents, such as bitter training sprays, be aware some dogs will not care if an item tastes bad—they will chew on it anyway. If you apply these deterrents, do not leave your dog alone and expect him to stop chewing. You should watch your dog's reaction before trusting that the bad habit is broken. Since some Westies have separation anxiety, you should eliminate the chewing problem as quickly as possible; this will allow your pup to roam freely around your home.

Jumping

As noted earlier, even though they are small, Westies shouldn't be allowed to jump up. Use the following steps when you have a visitor. If you can, get someone who is willing to help because that will make the training that much easier:

1. Put a leash on the dog when the person knocks on the door or rings the bell. The arrival of someone will invariably excite most dogs, especially puppies.

2. Let the person in, but do not approach him until your pup calms down.

3. Be effusive in your praise when the puppy keeps all four paws on the ground.

4. If the puppy jumps up on the visitor, the visitor should turn his body and ignore the dog. Don't verbally correct the dog. Being completely ignored will be far more of a deterrent than any words you can say.

5. Give your dog something to hold in his mouth if he does not settle down. Sometimes dogs just need a task to reduce their excitement. A stuffed animal or a ball is an ideal distraction, even if your dog drops it.

6. At this point, the visitor can get low and pet your dog. Having someone on his level will make your Westie feel he is being included. It also lets him sniff the visitor's face, which is part of a proper greeting to a dog. If your visitor is willing to help, this acknowledgment can prevent your pup from further jumping since he already feels safe with the person who is at his level.

Attention Seeking and Barking

If you are ignoring your Westie, he may act like toddlers and young children do, resorting to any means of getting your attention, even if that attention is negative. There can be different ways of acting out, like destroying something or barking. Since what he really wants is your attention, the best way to train him is by ignoring him when he acts out. If he is barking, don't acknowledge him. Once he stops barking, count to five, then praise your Westie for the quiet. If he destroys things, remove the items so he can do no harm.

Ignoring your dog is what works best when deterring attention-seeking behavior. As difficult as that may be, it is necessary to keep your puppy from learning how to push your buttons. After all, you do not want those behaviors to escalate when he is an adult. He will be able to do a lot more damage when he is older, and his voice will be a lot louder!

If you want to train your Westie to be a watchdog, you won't want to entirely discourage barking. You simply want to train him not to bark for attention just because he is bored.

Reward-Based Training Versus Discipline-Based Training

With an intelligent breed like the Westie, it is much more efficient to train your puppy using rewards than with punishments. This will be a particular challenge as puppies can be exuberant and are easily distracted. It is important to remember that your puppy is young, so you need to keep your temper and learn when a break from training is needed.

The following lists several critical training aspects you will need to address during the first month:

- House training (Chapter 10)
- Crate training (Chapter 6)
- Barking (Chapter 12)

Find out how much house training was completed by the breeder. The best breeders may teach puppies one or two commands before the puppy goes home with you. If this is the case, keep using those same commands with your puppy so that the early training is not lost. This information can help you establish the right tone of voice to use with your puppy since he will already know what the words mean and how to react to them.

Photo Courtesy
of Morag Swinton

How Long Is Too Long to Be Left Home Alone?

"There is a rule of sevens in raising puppies and most breeders are fa-miliar with early socialization. By the time a puppy is 7 weeks old, they should have been with 7 different people, eaten in 7 different containers, played with 7 different toys, etc....continue to expose your Westie puppy to different persons, places and things once they arrive home."

BONNIE SUE HURLEY
OakTree Kennels

In the beginning, your dog should spend only a brief period of time in the crate while you are gone. Though the breed is often independent, they are still pack animals. They do better when they have their pack than when they are left home alone for lengthy periods of time. Also, in those early days, your home is a new, potentially scary place.

As your dog becomes house trained and trustworthy, you should allow him to leave the crate while you are gone so that he doesn't feel he is being punished. Your new companion will not do well trapped in a crate for hours at a time.

You also need to find some good mental games that will keep your pup occupied while you are gone. Brain games can keep your dog happily occu-pied while you are away, and having another dog can provide stimulation (though you may want to make sure to tire them out before leaving if you have a couple of intelligent dogs, like the Westie).

If you are gone for several hours most days of the week, you should have a second dog to keep the Westie company. However, nothing is quite as good as having someone home most of the day. Work to overlap your day so that your Westie has someone to hang out with.

Don't Overdo It – Physically or Mentally

As an adult, your Westie will probably be highly active. As a puppy, your Westie will go from sleeping to being rambunctious to sleeping again, all within a brief period of time. A tired puppy is a lot like a tired toddler; you have to keep the little guy from becoming exhausted or from overworking those little legs. You need to be careful about harming your puppy's growing bones. Your pup is probably going to think that sleep is unnecessary, no matter how tired he is. It is up to you to read the signs that tell you when to stop all activities and to take a break or to put your pup to bed.

You should train your dog in increments of time—only for the amount of time that he can handle. Don't push your puppy's training past his concentration level, and don't discourage your adult dog by using commands that are too advanced. If you continue training your puppy past his energy levels, the lessons learned are not going to be the ones you want to teach your dog. At this age, training sessions don't need to be long; they just need to be consistent.

Walks will be much shorter during the first month. When you go outside, stay within a few blocks of home. Don't worry—by the month's end, your puppy will have more stamina, so you can enjoy longer walks with your new friend. You can also do a bit of walking on the leash in the yard if your puppy has lots of extra energy. Puppies have a tendency to attack their leash while walking because it is a distraction from running freely. Taking walks will also help your Westie learn how to behave on the leash.

Just because your puppy can't endure long walks initially doesn't mean he won't have plenty of energy. Daily exercise will be essential, with the caveats that you need to make sure your puppy isn't doing too much too soon and that he doesn't get too hot. Staying active will not only keep him healthy, but it will also keep him mentally stimulated. You will quickly realize how sedentary your "non-puppy life" has been because you will be on the move the entire time your puppy is awake!

CHAPTER 10
Housetraining

"Do not attempt to house train your puppy without a crate. The crate must be large enough for the puppy to stand up and sleep comfortably, but not too big. Westies will not want to be near their waste, so make sure they do not have enough space to sleep on one side and potty on the other. It only needs to be big enough to sleep in comfortably."

LEA LESLIE
Westiesworldforever

Even with the most trainable breed, house training is always a chore that ranks low on the list of things people want to do with their puppies. The good thing about Westies is that they loathe having a dirty space. As long as you keep your Westie in a small area when you aren't interacting with your puppy and do not take your eyes off the puppy when not in the area, house training is not that difficult. However, if you fail to keep a constant eye on your puppy, be prepared for a lot of messes. They are small as puppies, and they will sneak off to use the bathroom inside if you let your attention stray when they aren't in their designated area. This is a dog that can be stubborn, so you cannot give them a chance to get away with using your home as their bathroom.

This is where learning to be firm and consistent is really going to count, and sticking to the rules will be absolutely essential. You will also need to remain calm and patient; getting upset will only reinforce undesirable behavior. Your best tool in house training a potentially stubborn breed is to set a schedule and stick to it—no deviations!

Leashing your Westie to go outside can help show your puppy where and when to go to the bathroom – even in your yard. However, there will still be challenges as you try to convince your puppy the designated place for the bathroom is not inside your home!

The following is a list of rules to apply when house training:
- Never let the puppy roam the house alone—he should always be in his dedicated puppy space when you are not watching him. No Westie wants

to spend a lot of time in a soiled crate, so being in his crate is a deterrent from doing his business there when you are not around. He may not feel the same way about other areas of your home if he is free to wander.

- Give your puppy constant, easy access to his designated bathroom spaces. You will need to make frequent trips outside with your puppy as he learns where to do his business. When you go outside, put a leash on your puppy to make a point of where in the yard you want him to use the bathroom.

Always begin with a training plan; then be even stricter with yourself than you are with your puppy when keeping the schedule. You are the key to your puppy's learning!

Photo Courtesy
of Vernon Montoya

My Crate Training Strategy

Melanie Clark
Gap Kennels

Melanie Clark

In my opinion, crate training is the easiest way to house train a puppy. A dog is basically a "denning" animal, so a puppy will not be comfortable in being in his crate with any urine or feces. I would suggest a 24" training crate for a Westie puppy.

If you are not able to watch every move that your puppy makes, he should be in his crate. Therefore, he should be in his training crate unless you are holding him, playing with him, or feeding him, etc. until he is totally house trained. This is a very hard thing to do at first, but you will not regret being diligent and consistent.

For instance, if you are playing with him in your living room and you need to go cook, just take the crate in the kitchen with you and place him in it. You want the crate kept in an area where you physically are and not in another room, since the crate should not be used as a punishment. He will love his safe place.

I use the bell training system during the daytime. Each time I take the puppy out of his crate, I walk to the door, show him the bell as I ring it, and say "Do you want to go out?" If you ring the bell each time you take the puppy out, the puppy will realize very quickly that when you ring the bell, he goes outside. He will think, "they ring the bell and I go out, so if I ring the bell, they will let me out!"

Westies pick up very quickly on this training technique, and a new owner's consistency is the key.

At night, you will need to put the training crate on your nightstand, so the puppy can see you. This will make the puppy feel safe and secure, which will eliminate the whining of a new puppy during the night.

Let the puppy play well before you go to bed, so he will be tired and ready to sleep. After you put the puppy in the crate, touch him with your fingers through the wire, and the puppy will lay down. He feels loved, snuggled, and safe. If you hear your puppy wake up during the night, be very quiet and take the puppy outside, but just long enough to urinate.

You don't want your puppy to wake up and think it is "daytime play-time". After your puppy does his business, just put him back into the crate and put your fingers back through and touch him. He should go back to sleep for the rest of the night.

Consistency is the key.

*Photo Courtesy
of Morag Swinton*

Inside or Outside – House Training Options and Considerations

If your breeder has already started the house training process, make sure to coordinate your training so that you pick up where they left off. Having someone who really knows how to house train a dog can give you a huge leg up on the whole endeavor—take it if you can get it!

The following is a list of house training options for your puppy:

- Pee pads – You should have several around the home for training, including in the puppy's area but as far from his bed as possible.
- Regular outings – Organize these outings based on your puppy's sleeping and eating schedule.
- Rewards – You can use treats in the beginning but quickly shift to praise.

Setting a Schedule

"I use a timer to remind me how long it's been since the last time they were out. Their bladders are very small so 30 minutes is a god starting point, and then add or subtract as needed. At the alarm, I pick up the puppy and carry it to the potty place. A spot outside with artificial turf works well. Once they pee, I bring them back inside and reset the timer."

MARLEEN C BURFORD
MARDOT

You need to keep an eye on your puppy and always follow his meals and sleep with house-training sessions. Watch for cues like sniffing and circling, which are two common signs a puppy exhibits when searching for a place to go. Start tailoring your schedule around your puppy's unique needs.

Puppies have small bladders and little control in the early days—so at this time, it isn't stubbornness but ability that is making it difficult for your puppy to follow your directions. If you train your pup to do his business inside, you need a designated space in the puppy's area for a clean pee pad. Make sure you change the pads regularly so that your puppy does not get accustomed to having waste nearby. Pee pads are better than newspapers and can absorb more. Even if you use pee pads, you should plan to transition your dog to doing his business outdoors as quickly as possible.

Choosing a Location

"Using a consistent location can be key, the concentration of smells from the previous 'visits' will allow them to sniff and associate it with their previous actions. Also, if there is already another dog in the house, encourage your new Westie to follow that dog out to witness the potty process."

CHRISTOPHER LARSON
West Highland White Terrier

A designated bathroom space will make the house training experience easier because your Westie will associate one area of the yard for that specific purpose. Instead of sniffing around until he finds a choice spot, have him use one spot every time, which will also make cleanup simpler, and you will be able to use the entire yard instead of having to worry about stepping in dog waste.

The perfect time to train your puppy to go to the bathroom is when you go out for walks. Between walks and using the yard, your puppy will come to see the leash as a sign that it is time to relieve his bladder, which could become a Pavlovian response.

Do not send your puppy outside alone and assume he has done what you want him to do. He needs to understand the purpose of going outside is

Photo Courtesy of Edie Rosner

to go to the bathroom. Until there are no more accidents in the house, you need to be sure your puppy is not losing focus. With a breed like the Westie, it is best to always verify that your little fellow follows through. If it is too hot or cold outside, and you don't make sure he takes care of business, you run the risk that he will take advantage of that lack of supervision to pretend just so he can get back inside faster. Then accidents are nearly guaranteed, even if you thought that your dog was fully trained.

Key Word Training

All training should include key words, even house training. You and all family members should consistently use these key words when house training your dog. If you have paired an adult with a child, the adult should be the one using the key word during training.

To avoid confusing your puppy, be careful not to select words that you often use inside the home. Use a phrase like, "Get busy," to let your puppy know it's time to do his business. Do not use words like "bathroom" or "potty" because these words are sometimes used in casual conversation, which could trigger a desire to go to the bathroom. "Get busy" is not a phrase most people use in their daily routine, so it is not something you are likely to say unless you want your puppy to go to the bathroom outside.

Once your puppy learns to use the bathroom based on the command, make sure he finishes before offering praise or rewards.

HELPFUL TIP
Apartment-Friendly Pooch

Due to their smaller size and moderate energy level, Westies can be an excellent option for apartment dwellings. Training your Westie to use puppy pads can be a convenient option for you and your dog, especially if your apartment does not have access to a fenced yard. To encourage your dog to use puppy pads, you can purchase an attractant spray and place the pad in a place away from any main thoroughfares. In addition, using a puppy-pad holder is a great way to discourage your dog from chewing the pad and prevent the pad from slipping when your Westie uses it.

Reward Good Behavior with Positive Reinforcement

Positive reinforcement is highly effective. In the beginning, take a few pieces of kibble with you when you are teaching your puppy where to go, both inside and outside the home. Learning you are the one in charge will help teach your Westie to look to you for cues and instructions.

Part of being consistent with training means lavishing the little guy with praise whenever your puppy does the right thing. Use a leash to gently lead your puppy to his bathroom area, with no stops in between. It will gradually become obvious to your Westie this is where he should go to use the bathroom. Once you get outside, encourage your pup to go only when you get to the place in the yard that is intended for his bathroom spot. As soon as he does his business, give him immediate and very enthusiastic praise. Pet your puppy as you talk, and let the little guy know just how good the action was. Once the praise is done, return inside immediately. This is not playtime. You want your puppy to associate certain outings with designated potty time.

While praise is incredibly effective with Westies, you can also give your puppy a treat after a few successful trips outside. Definitely do not make treats a habit after each trip because you do not want your Westie to expect one every time he does his business. The lesson is to go outside, not to receive a treat every time.

The best way to house train in the first couple of months is to go out every hour or two, even during the night. Set an alarm to wake yourself during the night so that you remember to take the puppy outside. Use the leash to keep the focus on using the bathroom, give the same enthusiastic praise, then immediately return inside and go back to bed. It is difficult, but your Westie will get the hang of it a lot faster if there isn't a lengthy period between potty breaks. Over time, the pup will need to go outside less frequently.

Cleaning Up

Once a dog goes to the bathroom in your home, that odor will remain there for other dogs to smell, even if it's not detectable to your own nose after you've cleaned the area thoroughly. Your Westie might take any lingering odor as a sign that the spot is an acceptable place to use the bathroom.

Photo Courtesy
of Margaret Meroni

This means you have to be very diligent about handling accidents:

- Clean up any messes in the house as soon as you find them.
- In areas where your dog has an accident, thoroughly clean the spot so that there is no remaining scent.

Spend a bit of time researching what kinds of cleaner you want to use, whether generic or holistic. For example, you will likely want to get a product with an enzyme cleaner. Enzymes help to remove stains by speeding up the chemical reaction of the cleaner with the stain. They also help to remove the smell faster, which reduces the odds your dog will continue to go to the bathroom in the same place. If your Westie is properly trained, he will feel no need to mark his territory, but you should also discourage other dogs from claiming areas around your property.

If your Westie has an accident, it is important to refrain from punishing the puppy. Punishment simply teaches your dog to hide his mess or to be stealthier about when he goes inside. Accidents are not a reason to punish. If they happen often, it is really more of a reflection of your training and your schedule than on the puppy. However, even the best trainers can tell you accidents are pretty much an inevitability. When it happens, tell your puppy, "No! Potty outside!" and clean up the mess immediately. Once you have finished cleaning the mess, take the puppy outside. It isn't likely that he will need to go potty again, but it is worth the attempt in case he still has a little left.

Pay attention to when these accidents happen and determine if there is a commonality between them. Perhaps you need to add an extra trip outside during the day for your puppy, or you should make a change in his walking schedule. Maybe there is something that is startling your dog and causing an accident.

CHAPTER 11
Socialization

"Westies love the companionship of other dogs. They tend to bond very closely with other dogs in their home. Puppies should be socialized with other dogs at a young age, and dog friendships are important. Play dates with other pets is a great idea to ensure that your Westie is well socialized."

MELANIE CLARK
Gap Kennels

All dogs, regardless of breed, have to learn how to interact with other canines and humans, even dogs that tend to be friendly like Westies. You should create time in your schedule to ensure that your dog receives socialization to bring out those fantastic personality traits that are built into his genetics. If you begin socialization when your puppy is still young, he will learn that other dogs and people can be a lot of fun. Remember that your puppy will need to have all his vaccinations before being exposed to other dogs.

Keep in mind that terriers can be territorial, and that can include the Westie (though they are less territorial than most of their terrier relatives). You will need to monitor behavior closely in the early days to stop any territorial behavior for things like toys. It is best to avoid having food around during socialization sessions.

Another benefit of early socialization is that it can make life much more enjoyable for everyone involved, no matter what the situation. A socialized dog will approach the world from a much better place than a dog that is not socialized.

Greeting New People

Puppies will likely enjoy meeting new people, so make sure to invite friends over to help socialize your new canine family member. Your Westie may initially react by barking, but this likely will stop as soon as the person

tries to pet your pooch. Still, you will need to be careful to make sure that there are no territorial behaviors.

The following is a list of methods to use when introducing your puppy to a new person:

- Try to have your puppy meet new people daily, if possible. This could be during walks or while you are doing other activities, both inside and outside of the house. If you can't meet new people daily, try at least four times a week.

- Invite friends and family over and let them spend a few minutes giving the puppy their undivided attention. If your puppy has a favorite game or activity, let people know so they can play with him. This will win the little guy over very quickly and teach him new people are fun and safe to be around.

- Once your puppy is old enough to learn to do tricks (after the first month), have your little friend perform his tricks for visitors.

- Avoid crowds for the first few months. When your puppy is older, attend dog-friendly events so your pup can learn to be comfortable around a large group of people.

Greeting New Dogs

Chapter 8 explained how to introduce your new Westie to your other dogs. However, meeting dogs that are not part of your household is a little different, especially since you may encounter them at any time when you are out walking. The goal is to be able to walk around your neighborhood while your dog remains calm, refraining from running up to other dogs that may not be as friendly. The problem will likely be with the other dog, particularly if the other dog is not sociable; having a dog running toward it may be upsetting. Therefore, you need to train your Westie as early as possible to keep him safe.

Most dogs will bow and sniff each other during an introduction. Remember to watch for signs of aggression (Chapter 8), such as raised hackles and bared teeth. It is unlikely, but it is best to be safe. Bowing, high tail, and perked ears usually mean that your Westie is excited about meeting the other dog. If your Westie is making noises, make sure that the sounds are playful by paying attention to the physical reaction. This applies more if you adopted an adult than if you have a puppy, but it is always a good idea to keep an eye out regardless of the age of your dog.

The best way to help a Westie feel comfortable around unfamiliar dogs is to set up playdates with other dogs in a neutral place. This should make the whole experience much easier.

Don't let your Westie jump up on other dogs, no matter how excited he is. This action can become a way of showing dominance, which you really don't want with your puppy, even if it is just play in the beginning. If he does jump up, immediately say, "No," to let him know it is not acceptable behavior.

Photo Courtesy of Michele Brady

The Importance of Continuing Socialization

Even friendly dogs need socialization. When family and friends visit, encourage them to bring their dogs. This will remind your Westie his home is a welcoming place and not somewhere he needs to exert his dominance. You do not want your pup to think he can be a terror in his own house.

*Photo Courtesy
of The Grimsley Family*

Socializing an Adult Dog

Socializing an adult canine requires a lot of time, dedication, gentle training, and a firm approach. There's no guarantee that your dog will be happy being around other dogs. You may be lucky enough to get an adult that is already well-socialized. That does not mean you can remain entirely relaxed! Your new dog may have had a terrible experience with a particular breed of dog that no one knows about, and this can result in a bad situation.

Your dog should be adept at the following commands before you work on socialization:

- Sit
- Down
- Heel
- Stay

"Stay" is especially important because this demonstrates your dog has self-control by remaining in one place based on your command. This quality will be helpful when socializing because using this command will allow you to control your Westie in any situation. When you go outside, you will need to be very aware of your surroundings and be able to command your dog before another dog or person gets near.

Photo Courtesy
of Ann-Mary Cloutier

- Use a short leash on walks. Being aware of your surroundings will start to cue you in to what is making your dog react, so you can start training him not to react negatively.

- Change direction if you notice your Westie is not reacting well to a person or dog that is approaching. Avoidance is a good short-term solution until you know your dog is more accepting of the presence of other dogs or people.

HELPFUL TIP
Puppy Classes

Westies have a reputation for stubbornness, and while this is just part of your dog's multifaceted personality, it can help you both in the long term to introduce expectations at an early age. Early socialization is an excellent way to lay the foundation for a harmonious training relationship. Puppy socialization classes can usually begin when your puppy has finished his last round of vaccinations, between 12 and 16 weeks, and are offered at most big box pet stores as well as by privately operated trainers.

- If you are not able to take a different direction, tell your dog to sit, then block his view. This can prove to be particularly challenging as he will try to look around you. Continue to distract your dog so he will listen to you, taking his mind off what is coming toward him.

- Ask friends with friendly dogs to visit you, then meet in an enclosed space. Having one or two friendly dogs to interact with can help your Westie realize not all dogs are dangerous or need to be put in their place. When dogs wander around the area together, with no real interaction, your dog will learn that the others are enjoying the outside too. So, there is no reason to try to bully them!

- Get special treats for when you go walking. If your dog is aggressive when walking, have him sit and give him one of the special treats. Westies are food motivated, so this could be a perfect way of distracting your dog from whatever is making him feel protective. At the first snarl or sign of aggression, engage the training mentality and draw upon your dog's desire for those special treats. This method is slow, but it is reliable because your dog will learn that the appearance of strangers and other dogs means special treats for him. He will realize going on a walk is a positive experience, not a negative one. Nonetheless, this does not train him to interact with those dogs. Couple this tip with the previous suggestion to get the best results.

If you have ongoing problems with your adult dog, consult a behaviorist or specialized trainer.

CHAPTER 12

Training Your West Highland White Terrier

"A Westie has a great sense of humor and his whole ambition in life is to have fun! A Westie keeps his lively, "loving life" attitude well into his senior years. He loves to please others, but also has a mind of his own (and may even be stubborn at times). They are very intelligent and learn very quickly, so the new owner must be consistent with training, teaching their puppy what is acceptable and what is not from the very beginning."

MELANIE CLARK
Gap Kennels

Westies are popular because they can be easy to train. With the right incentives, most of them get over that stubborn streak because they would much rather have fun with you than just get their way. When weighing what they want against play, Westies almost universally prefer play and interaction.

In the early days, be prepared to keep your frustration levels in check. Your dog has to be convinced of the idea that you are in charge and that you mean business—and he needs to know the reward for that is a lot of fun. If you take out your frustration on your Westie, you are teaching him that training isn't fun. Whether you bring a puppy or an adult dog into the home, he has to learn the boundaries in a way that is safe and shows patience, just like with a child. If you take a few minutes to watch training videos of Westies from the beginning, that will give you a good idea of what you could be in for when you start to train your newest family member.

Just remember—being firm, consistent, and patient will go a long way. Don't let that adorable face sway you from getting your pup to do what you instruct him to do. Remember, he will be just as happy a little ways down the road if you stick to it now. And those happy faces when playing with you are priceless.

Always make the early training sessions short, no matter how old your dog is. Those training sessions are as much about learning how your Westie will respond to training as they are about actually training. Puppies won't have the ability to keep focus like an adult, so a short session is ideal for keeping them from learning to ignore you. Adult dogs are going to be suspicious of you (though you may also get an adult that is already familiar with training, which could make training a little easier). And odds are, you are going to be quite tired by the end of those sessions—you'll be just as relieved as your pup to be done. As long as you are firm and consistent during those early sessions, keeping them short is in everyone's best interest.

Training will be slow going in the beginning as your dog will be quite excited for the interaction. Don't take this as an indication of your puppy's interest levels—it's more indicative of his inexperience. If you are patient with your pup from the start, you will find it will pay off later.

Photo Courtesy
of Alex and Ethan Wright

Benefits of Proper Training

Training is as important as socialization, and it can make general excursions easier; more importantly, training could be a way of saving your dog's life. Understanding commands might prevent your dog from running into the street, from responding to provocations from other dogs, or from acting territorially.

Training can also really benefit your relationship with your pup because it is a wonderful way to bond. This dedicated time together helps you understand your puppy's developing personality as you learn what kind of reward will work best for other tasks. Be sure your Westie is well-trained so you can enjoy a full range of activities together—from picnics to outings in the park!

Photo Courtesy of Amelia Barrable

Choosing the Right Reward

The right reward for a Westie will ultimately be love and affection because they adore their people. Treats are the easiest way of keying a puppy into the idea that performing tricks is good behavior, but ultimately you want your little one to follow commands without expecting food. Soon, you will need to switch to a reward that is a secondary reinforcer. Praise, additional playtime, and extra petting are all fantastic rewards for your Westie. Your dog will probably follow you around until you decide to just sit back and relax. Plopping down to watch a movie and letting your puppy sit with you is a great reward after an intense training session. Not only did your puppy learn, but you both now get to relax together.

Because this is a smaller breed, you need to be careful about overfeeding your dog, and that includes treats. Make sure you switch to a different kind of positive reward as early as possible. Since many Westies love their toys, you don't have to rely solely on treats as a method of praise.

If you would like your Westie to connect positive feedback with a sound, you can use a clicker. This training tool is relatively inexpensive and should be used at the same time as you praise your puppy or dog. Clickers are not necessary, but some trainers find them useful.

Name Recognition

Over time, many of us create different names for our dogs. Nicknames, joke names, and descriptions based on some of their ridiculous actions can all be used later. However, before you can train a dog, you have to make sure he understands his real name.

The following list gives some name recognition suggestions:

1. Get some treats and show one to your dog.
2. Say the dog's name and immediately say, "Yes." (Your dog should be looking at you when you speak.) Then, give your dog a treat.
3. Wait ten seconds, then show your dog a treat and repeat step two.

Sessions shouldn't last longer than about five minutes because your dog will lose focus or interest. Name recognition is something you can do several times each day. After you have done this for five to ten sessions, the training will change a bit:

1. Wait until your dog isn't paying attention to you.

② Call your dog. If he has a leash on, give it a gentle tug to get your dog's attention.

③ Say, "Yes," and give the dog a treat when he looks at you.

During this time, do not speak your dog's name when you correct him or for any reason other than name recognition. This is because, in the beginning, you need to get the dog to associate his name only with something positive, like treats. This will more quickly program your dog to listen to you no matter what else is going on around him.

It is likely that your Westie will not require a lot of time before he recognizes his name. Repetition while looking at your pup is a great way to speed up that learning process.

Photo Courtesy
of Roy Poh

Essential Commands

"Westies are high energy and easily distracted. Regular exercise and patience is a must during training. Work on one command at a time, for only a few minutes. And always reward with treats and praise."

NORA BALIN STONE
Balinbrae Westies

There are six basic commands that all dogs should know (Sit, Down, Stay, Come, Leave It, and Drop It). These commands are the basis for a happy and enjoyable relationship with your dog, as well as giving you a way to keep your dog safe and out of trouble. Then there are some commands that are incredibly helpful, like Off if you don't want pets on the furniture and Quiet for a noisy dog.

Train your puppy to do the commands in the order they appear in this chapter. The last two are optional since you may allow your dog on the furniture, and he may not be a particularly vocal canine. Since dogs sit often, it is the easiest command to teach, making it the best starting point. Teaching Leave It and Drop It is much more difficult and usually requires the puppy to fight an instinct or a desire. Consider how much you give in to something you want—when you know you shouldn't! That's pretty much what your puppy is facing.

Quiet can be another difficult command as dogs (particularly puppies) tend to bark in response to their surroundings. However, you don't have to teach it right from the beginning, as some puppies do grow out of the constantly barking stage. If you finish all of the other commands and find that your dog is still a bit too noisy for your home, you

HELPFUL TIP
Dealing with Digging

Most dogs will dabble in digging at some point in their lives, but for West Highland White Terriers, digging may be a more prevalent issue. This behavior may stem from the fact that Westies were initially bred to hunt rodents and small game, but this penchant for digging may be less than ideal in the modern backyard (or living room!). Additionally, excessive digging may result from a lack of physical or mental exercise, so be sure that your dog is getting sufficient stimulation throughout the day. Finally, if your dog is still engaging in destructive digging even with proper exercise, try utilizing known commands with your dog, such as "come," to disrupt the behavior.

can then start training, though you will need to determine just when you want them to be quiet and when you want them to bark (like when someone is outside your home). This will take some consideration on your part before you begin.

The following are some basic steps to use during training:

1. Include everyone in the home in the Westie training. The puppy must learn to listen to everyone in the household and not just one or two people. A set training schedule may only involve a couple of people in the beginning, especially if you have children. There should always be an adult present when training, but including a child will help reinforce the idea that the puppy must listen to everyone in the house. It is also an effective way for a parent to monitor a child's interaction with the puppy so that everyone plays in a way that is safe and that follows the rules.

2. To get started, select an area where you and your puppy have no other distractions, including noise. Leave your phone and other devices out of range so that you are able to keep your attention on the puppy.

3. Stay happy and excited about the training. Your puppy will pick up on your enthusiasm and will focus better because of it.

4. Be consistent and firm as you teach.

5. Bring a special treat to the first few training sessions, such as pieces of chicken or small treats.

Sit

Start to teach the command Sit when your puppy is around eight weeks old.

Once you settle into your quiet training location:

1. Hold out a treat.
2. Move the treat over your puppy's head. This will make the puppy move back.
3. Say, "Sit" as the puppy's haunches touch the floor.

Having a second person around to demonstrate this with your puppy will be helpful as they can sit to show the dog what you mean.

Wait until your puppy starts to sit down and say, "Sit" as he sits. If your puppy finishes sitting down, give praise. Naturally, this will make your puppy excited and wiggly, so it may take a bit of time before he will want to sit again. When your puppy calms down, repeat the process.

It's going to take more than a couple of sessions for the puppy to fully connect your words with the actions. Commands are something completely new to your little companion. Once your puppy has demonstrated mastery of the command Sit, start teaching Down.

Down

Repeat the same process when teaching this command as you did for Sit:

(1) Tell your dog to Sit.

(2) Hold out the treat.

(3) Lower the treat to the floor with your dog sniffing at it. Allow your pup to lick the treat, but if he stands up, start over.

(4) Say, "Down" as the puppy's elbows touch the floor (make sure to say it as he does the action to help him associate the word with the action), then give praise while rewarding your puppy with the treat.

It will probably take a little less time to teach this command. Wait until your puppy has mastered Down before moving on to Stay.

Stay

Stay is a vital command to teach because it can keep your puppy from running across a street or from running at someone who is nervous or scared of dogs. It is important your dog has mastered Sit and Down before you teach Stay. Learning this command is going to be more difficult since it is not something your puppy does naturally.

Be prepared for this command to take a bit longer to teach:

(1) Tell your puppy to either Sit or Stay.

(2) As you do this, place your hand in front of the puppy's face.

(3) Wait until the puppy stops trying to lick your hand before you continue.

(4) When the puppy settles down, take a step away. If your puppy is not moving, say, "Stay," and give a treat and some praise.

Giving your puppy the reward indicates the command is over, but you also need to indicate the command is complete. The puppy has to learn to stay until you say it is okay to leave the spot. Once you give the okay to move, do not give treats. The command Come should not be used as the okay word, as it is a command used for something else.

Repeat these steps, taking more steps further away from the puppy after a successful command.

Once your puppy understands Stay when you move away, start training him to Stay even if you are not moving. Extend the amount of time required for the puppy to stay in one spot so that he understands Stay ends with the Okay command.

When you feel that your puppy has Stay mastered, start training the puppy to Come.

Come

This is a command you can't teach until the puppy has learned the previous commands. Before you start the training session, decide if you want to use Come or Come Here. Be consistent in the words you use.

This command is important for the same reason as the previous one; if you are around people who are nervous around dogs, or if you encounter a wild animal or other distraction, this command will snap your puppy's attention back to you:

(1) Leash the puppy.

(2) Tell the puppy to Stay.

(3) Move away from the puppy.

(4) Say the command you will use for Come and give a gentle tug on the leash toward you.

Repeat these steps, building a larger distance between you and the puppy. Once the puppy seems to understand, remove the leash, and start at a close distance. If your puppy doesn't seem to understand the command, give some visual clues about what you want. For example, you can pat your leg or snap your fingers. As soon as your puppy comes running over to you, offer a reward.

Leave It

This is a difficult training command, but you need to train your dog to Leave It for when you are out on a walk and want him to ignore other people or dogs.

(1) Let your dog see that you have treats in your hand, then close your hand. Your fist should be close enough for your dog to sniff the treat.

Photo Courtesy
of Letty Zemaitis

(2) Say, "Leave it" when your dog starts to sniff your hand.

(3) Say, "Yes," and give your dog a treat when he turns his head away from the treats. Initially, this will probably take a while, as your dog will want those treats. Don't continue to say, "Leave it," as your dog should not be learning that you will give a command more than once. You want him to learn he must do what you say the first time, which is why treats are recommended in the beginning. If a minute or more passes after giving the command, you can then issue it again, but make sure your canine is focused on you and not distracted.

These sessions should only last about five minutes. Your dog will need time to learn this command as you are teaching him to ignore something he does naturally. When he looks away and stops sniffing when you say, "Leave it," you can move on to more advanced versions of the training:

(1) Leave your hand open so that your dog can see the treats.

(2) Say, "Leave it" when your dog starts to show interest. This will probably be immediate since your hand will be open, so be prepared.
   a. Close your fist if your dog continues to sniff or gets near the treats in your hand.
   b. Give your dog a treat from your other hand if he stops.

Repeat these steps until your dog finally stops trying to sniff the treats. When your dog seems to have this down, move on to the most difficult version of this command.

(1) Place treats on the ground or let your dog see you hide them. Then, stay close to those treats.

(2) Say, "Leave it" when your dog starts to show interest in sniffing the treats.
   a. Place a hand over the treats if he doesn't listen.
   b. Give a treat if your dog does listen.

From here, you can start training while standing further from the treat with your dog leashed, so you can stop him if needed. Then, start to use other things that your dog loves, such as a favorite toy or another tempting treat that you don't usually give him.

Drop It

This is going to be one of the most difficult commands to teach because it goes against both your puppy's instincts and interests. Your puppy wants to keep whatever he has, so you are going to have to offer him something better instead. It is essential to teach the command early, as your Westie

115

could be very destructive in the early days. Furthermore, this command could save your pooch's life. When you are out for a walk, he will likely lunge at objects that look like food. However, once he has mastered this command, he will drop anything he picks up.

Start with a toy and a treat or a large treat that your dog cannot eat in a matter of seconds, such as a rawhide. Make sure the treat you have is one your puppy does not get very often so that there is motivation to drop the toy or big treat.

1. Give your puppy the toy or large treat. If you want to use a clicker, too, pair it with the exciting treat you will use to help convince your puppy to drop the treat.

2. Show your puppy the exciting treat.

3. Say, "Drop it," and when he drops the treat or toy, tell him, "Good," and hand over the exciting treat while picking up the dropped item.

4. Repeat this immediately after your puppy finishes eating the exciting treat.

You will need to keep reinforcing this command for months after it is learned because it is not a natural instinct.

Off

This is different from training your dog not to jump on people (Chapter 9). This command is specifically to get your dog off furniture or surfaces that may be dangerous. This is training you will need to do on the fly because you are training your dog to stop an action. This means you have to react to that undesirable action. Having treats on hand will be essential when you see your dog getting up on things you don't want him to be on:

1. Wait for your dog to put his paws on something you don't want him on.

2. Say, "Off," and lure him away with a treat that you keep just out of his reach.

3. Say, "Yes," and give him a treat as soon as his paws are off the surface.

Repeat this every time you see the behavior. It will likely take at least half a dozen times before your dog understands he should not perform the action anymore. Over time, switch from treats to praise or playing with a toy.

Quiet

Westies tend to be rather quiet, but if you have a puppy that tends to bark, you may want to train the pup not to bark too often. Initially, you can use treats sparingly to reinforce quiet if your pup enjoys making noise:

(1) When your puppy barks for no obvious reason, tell him to be quiet and place a treat nearby. It is almost guaranteed your dog will fall silent to sniff the treat.

(2) If your dog does fall silent, say, "Good dog" or "Good quiet."

It will not take too long for your puppy to understand Quiet means no barking.

If you want your Westie to be more of a watchdog, you will need to provide some guidance on when he should bark. He will likely bark at the door when someone is there, so it won't be as difficult to teach him to bark for other reasons as well. A professional can help tailor the approach to training your dog when to bark at people at the door. Otherwise, you will want your dog to know he shouldn't be randomly barking at birds at the window or squirrels running around in the yard.

Until all of these commands are learned, it is best to avoid other types of advanced training. Between six and twelve months, you should be able to move on to tricks. Chapter 14 provides more details on tricks and games that your Westie may love.

Where to Go from Here

"Expose your Westie to loud noises, unusual surfaces, and unusual smells early on. Let them learn to be brave, but not aggressive. That is why a group training class is good; it's a perfect way to do this in a controlled atmosphere."

MARLEEN C BURFORD
MARDOT

Training doesn't have to be something you do on your own. There are several different types of classes you can enroll your Westie of any age in to help you feel more confident in your training abilities. Chapter 14 provides alternatives to helping your dog use up all of his energy, but you do need to at least ensure that your dog learns the basics. The following classes can help.

Puppy Classes

Puppies can begin to go to puppy school as early as six weeks. You will need to set aside an hour or two so that you can research schools near you. Make sure to take the time to read the reviews and see if you can talk to people who have used a particular school or trainer. Trainers should be willing to take the time to talk to you and answer questions as well, so try talking to the people running the school. This is the beginning of obedience training, but you need to be careful around other dogs until your puppy has completed his vaccinations. Talk with your vet about when is an appropriate time to begin classes. Your vet may be able to recommend good puppy training classes in your area.

The primary purpose of these classes is socialization. Studies show one-third of all puppies have minimal exposure to unfamiliar people and dogs during the first twenty weeks of their life. This can make the outside world pretty scary! The puppy classes give you and your puppy a chance to learn how to meet and greet other people and dogs in a controlled environment. Dogs that attend these classes are much friendlier and are less stressed about such things as large trucks, thunder, loud noises, and unfamiliar visitors. They are also less likely to be nervous or suffer from separation anxiety, a likely issue for a Westie.

Puppy classes are also great training for you! The same studies show owners who attend classes learn to react appropriately when their puppy is disobedient or misbehaves. The classes teach you how to train your puppy and how to deal with the emerging headstrong nature of your dog.

Many classes will help you with some of the basic commands, like Sit and Down. Look for a class that also focuses on socialization so that your puppy can get the most out of the instruction.

Obedience Training

"Westies are smart. When you begin obedience training a Westie you must remember when the Westie understands the command sit and does it, don't overdo repetition. Your Westie will get bored and look at you like you smell bad. Short training periods are best moving on to another command, after the first is accomplished."

BONNIE SUE HURLEY
OakTree Kennels

119

After your puppy graduates from puppy school and understands most of the basic commands, you can switch to obedience classes. Some trainers offer at-home obedience training, but if you do this, it's still a good idea to also set aside regular time to socialize your pup at a dog park. If your Westie attends puppy classes, the trainers there can recommend classes at the next level of training. Dogs of nearly any age can attend obedience training classes, although your dog should be old enough to listen to commands before instruction begins.

Obedience training usually includes the following:

- Teaching or reinforcing basic commands, like Sit, Stay, Come, and Down.
- How to walk without pulling on the leash.
- How to properly greet people and dogs, including not jumping on them.

Obedience school is as much about training you as training your dog. It helps you learn how to train your puppy while teaching your dog basic commands and how to behave for basic tasks, like greetings and walking. Classes usually last between seven and ten weeks.

Ask your vet for recommendations, and also consider the following when evaluating trainers:

- Are they certified, particularly the CPDT-KA certification?
- How many years have they been training dogs?
- Do they have experience with training Westies?
- Can you participate in the training? If the answer is no, do not use that trainer. You have to be a part of your dog's training because the trainer won't be around for most of your dog's life. Therefore, your dog has to learn to listen to you.

If your dog has anxiety, depression, or other serious behavioral problems, you need to hire a trainer to help your dog work through those issues. Do your research to be sure your trainer is an expert—preferably one with experience training intelligent, strong-willed dogs.

Once your Westie understands the basic commands and has done well in obedience training, you will know if more difficult training is right for him.

CHAPTER 13
Nutrition

Westies tend to be pretty picky eaters, so it should be easier to help your dog stay at a healthier weight. However, they are still small dogs, so you want to make sure that your dog doesn't overindulge in unhealthy foods because it won't take much for him to gain weight. This is why you want to switch from training with treats to praise. It is far too easy to give your dog too many treats. If everyone becomes accustomed to training the dog with praise or toys instead of treats, your dog's weight will be less problematic.

It's a good thing that they tend to be picky eaters because Westies are known to have sensitive stomachs. Selecting hypoallergenic food and being very selective about what foods you give your dog will definitely help him to live longer and have fewer stomach issues.

Why a Healthy Diet is Important

"A Westie's health depends a lot on their dog food. This is one area you should not be cheap on, a healthy Westie is a happy Westie. Westies naturally have dry skin, so adding a little coconut oil or fish oil will help with seasonal changes in dryness."

LEA LESLIE
Westiesworldforever

Just because your Westie is active doesn't mean he is burning all the calories he takes in, especially if you have an open treat policy. Just as you should not be eating all day, your puppy shouldn't be either. If you have a busy schedule, it will be too easy for your dog to have substantial lapses in activity levels while you are not ensuring the recommended daily exercise (covered in Chapter 14).

You need to be aware of roughly how many calories your dog eats a day, including treats, so be mindful of your dog's weight and whether or not he is putting on pounds. This will tell you if you should adjust his food intake or if you should change the food to something more nutritious and with fewer calories.

Always talk with your vet if you have concerns about your Westie's weight.

Dangerous Foods

Dogs can eat raw meat without having to worry about the kinds of problems a person would encounter. However, there are some human foods that could be fatal to your Westie.

The following is a list of foods you should **NEVER** feed your dog:

- Apple seeds
- Chocolate
- Coffee
- Cooked bones (They can kill a dog when the bones splinter in the dog's mouth or stomach.)
- Corn on the cob (The cob is deadly to dogs; corn off the cob is fine.)
- Grapes/raisins
- Macadamia nuts
- Onions and chives
- Peaches, persimmons, and plums
- Tobacco (Your Westie will not realize it is not a food and may eat it if it's left out.)
- Xylitol (a sugar substitute in candies and baked goods)
- Yeast

*Photo Courtesy
of Meghan Jackson*

In addition to this list, consult the Canine Journal for a lengthy list of other dangerous foods. (http://www.caninejournal.com/foods-not-to-feed-dog/)

CANINE NUTRITION

Canines are largely carnivorous, and protein is a significant dietary need. However, they need more than just protein to be healthy.

The following table provides the primary nutritional requirements for dogs:

Nutrient	Sources	Puppy	Adult
Protein	Meat, eggs, soybeans, corn, wheat, peanut butter	22.0% of diet	18.0% of diet
Fats	Fish oil, flaxseed oil, canola oil, pork fat, poultry fat, safflower oil, sunflower oil, soybean oil	8.0 to 15.0% of diet	5.0 to 15.0% of diet
Calcium	Dairy, animal organ tissue, meats, legumes (typically beans)	1.0% of diet	0.6% of diet
Phosphorus	Meat and pet supplements	0.8% of diet	0.5% of diet
Sodium	Meat, eggs	0.3% of diet	0.06% of diet

The following are the remaining nutrients dogs require, all of them less than 1% of a puppy or an adult diet:

- Arginine
- Histidine
- Isoleucine
- Leucine
- Lysine
- Methionine + cystine
- Phenylalanine + tyrosine
- Threonine
- Tryptophan
- Valine
- Chloride

It is best to avoid giving your dog human foods with a lot of sodium and preservatives. Water is also absolutely essential to keep your dog healthy. There should always be water in your dog's water bowl, so make a habit of checking it several times a day so that your dog does not get dehydrated.

Proteins and Amino Acids

Since dogs are carnivores, protein is one of the most important nutrients in a healthy dog's diet. (Dogs should not eat as much meat as their close wolf relatives do. Dogs' diets and needs have changed significantly since they have become human companions.) Proteins contain the necessary amino acids for your dog to produce glucose, which is essential for giving your dog energy. A lack of protein in your dog's diet will result in him being lethargic. His coat may start to look dull, and he is likely to lose weight. Conversely, if your dog gets too much protein, his body will store the excess protein as fat, and he will gain weight.

Meat is the best source of protein for your dog, and a dog's dietary needs are significantly different from a human's needs. If you plan to feed your dog a vegetarian diet, it is very important that you talk to your vet first. It is incredibly difficult to ensure that a carnivore receives adequate protein while on a vegetarian diet. Puppies in particular need to have adequate protein to be healthy adults, so you may need to give your puppy a diet with meat, then switch to a vegetarian diet after your Westie becomes an adult.

Fat and Fatty Acids

Most fats that your dog needs are found in meat. Seed oils provide a lot of necessary healthy fats, too, with peanut butter being one of the most common sources. Fats break down into fatty acids, which your dog needs for fat-soluble vitamins that help with regular cell functions. Perhaps the most obvious benefit of fats and fatty acids can be seen in your dog's coat. Your dog's coat will look and feel much healthier when your dog is getting the right nutrients.

The following is a list of potential health issues that might arise if your dog does not get adequate fats in his daily diet:

- His coat will look less healthy.
- His skin may be dry and itchy.
- His immune system could be compromised, making it easier for your dog to get sick.
- He may have an increased risk of heart disease. The primary concern if your dog gets too much fat is that he will become obese, leading to additional health problems.

Carbohydrates and Cooked Foods

Dogs have been living with humans for millennia, so their dietary needs have evolved like our own. They can eat foods with carbohydrates to supplement the energy typically provided by proteins and fats. If you cook grains (such as barley, corn, and rice) prior to feeding them to your dog, it will be easier for him to digest those complex carbohydrates. If your dog is allergic to grains, potatoes and sweet potatoes are also high in carbohydrates.

Different Dietary Requirements for Different Life Stages

"Feed a quality food at least twice daily for adults and four times daily for a puppy. Place the food in front of the Westie for 15 minutes then remove until the next feeding time. I have found a small topping of canned or 'wet' food encourages the Westie to begin eating. Although the definitive word is still out I have found that grain free diets are not the best for Westies. It is generally agreed they are lacking in an enzyme that promotes heart health in Westies."

BONNIE SUE HURLEY
OakTree Kennels

Different stages of a dog's life have different nutritional needs.

Puppy Food

During roughly the first twelve months of their lives, puppies' bodies are growing. To be healthy, they need more calories and have different nutritional needs to promote growth, so feed them a food made specifically for puppies. Puppies can have up to four meals a day. Just be careful not to overfeed them, particularly if you use treats during training. Their nutritional needs are much different than their adult counterparts.

Adult Dog Food

The primary difference between puppy food and adult dog food is puppy food is higher in calories and nutrients, which promote growth. Dog food manufacturers reduce these nutrients in adult dog food as they no longer need lots of calories to sustain growth. As a rule, when a canine reaches about 90% of his predicted adult size, you should switch to adult dog food.

The size of your Westie is key in determining how much to feed him. The following table is a general recommendation for daily food consumption for your adult Westie. Initially, you may want to focus on the calories as you try to find the right balance for your dog.

Dog Size	Calories per day
10 lbs.	420 during hot months
	630 during cold months
20 lbs.	700 during hot months
	1,050 during cold months

You can feed your Westie two or three times a day, so you can divide up the calories according to this schedule. Keep in mind these recommendations are per day and not per meal. To make sure your dog feels like a real part of the family, let your pup eat when you do, even if he doesn't get that much food at a time.

If you plan to add wet food, pay attention to the total calorie intake, and adjust how much you feed your dog between the kibble and wet food. The total calories in the kibble and wet food should balance out so as not to exceed your dog's needs. The same is true if you give your dog a lot of treats over the course of the day. You should factor treat calories into how much you feed your dog at mealtimes.

If you feed your dog homemade food (discussed later in this chapter), you should learn your nutrition facts, and you should pay close attention to calories instead of cup measurements.

Photo Courtesy
of Maxine Middleton

Senior Dog Food

Senior dogs are not always capable of being as active as they were in their younger days. If you notice your dog is slowing down or suffers joint pain and shows a lack of stamina when taking long walks, you can assume your Westie is entering his senior years. Consult with your vet if you think it is time to change the type of food you feed him.

The primary difference between adult and senior dog food is senior dog food contains less fat and more antioxidants to help fight weight gain. Senior dogs also need more protein, which will probably make your dog happy because that usually means more meat. Protein helps to maintain your dog's aging muscles. He should also be eating less phosphorus during his golden years to avoid the risk of developing hyperphosphatemia. This is a condition where dogs have excessive amounts of phosphorus in their bloodstream, and older dogs are at greater risk of developing it. The level of phosphorus in the body is controlled by the kidneys; as such, elevated levels of phosphorus are usually an indication of a problem with the kidneys.

Senior dog food has the correct number of calories for reduced activity, which means no adjustment of quantity is needed unless you notice weight gain. Consult your vet if you notice your dog is putting on weight because this could be a sign of illness.

Your Dog's Meal Options

"Westies need a well balanced diet. Some people think that a grain free diet is best for West Highland White Terriers. But some researchers have the opinion that grain free dog foods can cause heart problems in dogs due to the legumes, etc. found in the grain free foods. I do not personally feel that grain free is necessary for a Westie, unless you have experienced some skin allergy issue. No matter what type of food you choose, make sure the company uses wholesome ingredients and lists the main ingredient as meat."

MELANIE CLARK
Gap Kennels

You have three primary choices for what to feed your dog, or you can use a combination of the three, depending on your situation and your dog's specific needs.

Commercial Food

Make sure that you are buying the best dog food you can afford. Take the time to research each of your options, particularly the nutritional value of the food, and review this annually. Make sure the food you are giving your dog is high quality, and always take into account your dog's size, energy levels, and age. Your puppy may not need puppy food for as long as other breeds, and dog food for seniors may not be necessary for Westies. You'll need to pay attention to your dog's individual needs to determine if he needs a special food for his age.

The website Pawster provides several great articles about which commercial dog foods are best for Westies. Since new foods frequently come on the market, check periodically to see if there are new, better foods that have become available.

If you aren't sure which brand of food is best, talk with the breeder about the foods they recommend. Breeders are really the best guides for you here, as they are experts, but you can also ask your vet.

Some dogs may be picky eaters who get tired of repeatedly eating the same food. While you shouldn't frequently change the brand of food because that can upset your dog's stomach, you can get foods that have assorted flavors. You can also change the taste by adding a bit of wet (canned) food. Adding one-fourth to one-third of a can for each meal is an easy change to make to ensure your dog's happiness.

For more details on commercial options, check out the website Dog Food Advisor. They provide reviews on various dog food brands, as well as providing information on recalls and contamination issues.

COMMERCIAL DRY FOOD

Dry dog food often comes in bags, and it is what the vast majority of people feed their dogs.

Dry Dog Food

PROS	CONS
• Convenience	• Requires research to ensure you don't buy doggie junk food
• Variety	
• Availability	• Packaging is not always honest
• Affordability	• Recalls for food contamination
• Manufacturers follow nutritional recommendations (not all of them follow this, so do your brand research before you buy)	• Loose FDA nutritional regulations
	• Low quality food may have questionable ingredients
• Specially formulated for different canine life stages	
• Can be used for training	
• Easy to store	

The convenience and ease on your budget mean you are almost certainly going to buy kibble for your dog. This is perfectly fine, and most dogs will be more than happy to eat kibble. Be sure you know what brand you are feeding your dog, and pay attention to kibble recalls so you can stop feeding your dog a certain brand if necessary. Check out the following sites regularly for recall information:

- Dog Food Recalls – www.dogfoodadvisor.com
- American Kennel Club – www.AKC.org
- Dog Food Guide – www.dogfood.guide

COMMERCIAL WET FOOD

Most dogs prefer wet dog food over kibble, but it is also more expensive. Wet dog food can be purchased in large packs that can be extremely easy to store.

Wet Dog Food

PROS	CONS
• Helps keep dogs hydrated	• Dog bowls must be washed after every meal
• Has a richer scent and flavor	
• Easier to eat for dogs with dental problems (particularly those missing teeth) or if a dog has been ill	• Can soften bowel movements
	• Can be messier than kibble
	• Once opened, it has a short shelf-life and should be covered and refrigerated
• Convenient and easy to serve	
• Unopened, it can last between one and three years	• More expensive than dry dog food and comes in small quantities
• Balanced based on current pet nutrition recommendations	
	• Packaging is not always honest
	• Recalls for food contamination
	• Loose FDA regulations

Like dry dog food, wet dog food is convenient, and picky dogs are much more likely to eat it than kibble. If your dog gets sick, use wet dog food to ensure that he is still eating and gets the necessary nutrition each day. It may be harder to switch back to kibble once your Westie is healthy, but you can always add a little wet food to make each meal more appetizing.

Raw Diet

For dogs prone to food allergies, raw diets can help prevent an allergic reaction to wheat and processed foods. Raw diets are heavy in raw meats, bones, vegetables, and specific supplements. Some of the benefits of a raw diet include:

• Improves your dog's coat and skin
• Improves immune system

- Improves health (as a result of better digestion)
- Increases energy
- Increases muscle mass

Raw diets are meant to give your dog the kind of food canines ate before being domesticated. It means giving your dog uncooked meats, whole (uncooked) bones, and a small amount of dairy products. It doesn't include processed food of any kind—not even food cooked in your kitchen.

There are potential risks to this diet. Dogs have been domesticated for millennia, and their digestive systems have also evolved. Trying to force them to eat the kind of diet they ate hundreds of years ago does not always work as intended, primarily because they may not be able to fully digest raw food the way their ancestors did.

There are also many risks associated with feeding dogs uncooked meals, particularly if the food has been contaminated. Things like bacteria pose a serious risk and can be transferred to you if your dog gets sick. Many medical professionals also warn about the dangers of giving dogs bones even if they are uncooked. Bones can splinter in your dog's mouth and puncture the esophagus or stomach.

The Canine Journal (www.caninejournal.com) provides a lot of information about a raw diet, including different recipes and how to transition your dog to this diet. Always talk to your veterinarian before putting your dog on a new kind of diet.

Homemade Diet

The best home-cooked meals should be planned in advance so that your Westie gets the correct nutritional balance. Typically, 50 percent of your dog's food should be animal protein (fish, poultry, and organ meats). About 25 percent should be full of complex carbohydrates. The remaining 25 percent should be from fruits and vegetables, particularly foods like pumpkin, apples, bananas, and green beans. These foods provide extra flavor your Westie will probably love while filling him up faster and reducing the chance of overeating.

The following are a few sites where you can learn how to make homemade meals for canines. Most of them are not breed-specific, so if you have more than one dog, these meals can be made for all your furry canine friends:

- The Westie Diet: Recipes from the Rescue Kitchen (http://www.westierescuecalifornia.com/the_westie_diet)

- Hublore (http://hublore.blogspot.com/2011/05/homemade-dog-food-recipe.html)
- Homemade Dog Food with a Special Ingredient (https://pethelpful.com/dogs/Homemade-Dog-Food-with-an-Extra-Special-Ingredient)
- Canine Journal (https://www.caninejournal.com/homemade-dog-food-recipes/)
- DIY Homemade Dog Food (https://damndelicious.net/2015/04/27/diy-homemade-dog-food/)

Keep in mind the foods your Westie absolutely should not eat. You can also mix some of the food you make for yourself into your Westie's meal. Do not feed your Westie from your plate! Split the food, placing your dog's meal into a bowl so that your canine understands your food is just for you.

Scheduling Meals

Your Westie will likely expect you to stick to a schedule, which definitely includes mealtimes. If treats and snacks are something you establish as a normal routine, your dog will expect that too!

For puppies, plan to have three or four meals, while adults and seniors should typically have two meals a day.

Food Allergies and Intolerance

Whenever you start your dog on a new type of food (even if it's simply a different flavor), you need to monitor him while he becomes accustomed to the change. Food allergies are fairly common in Westies, and the symptoms manifest themselves as hot spots, which are similar to rashes in humans. Your dog may start scratching or chewing specific spots on his body, and his fur could start falling out around those spots.

FUN FACT
Cesar Spokesdog

Cesar Dog Food is easily recognizable for its adorable spokesdog, a West Highland White Terrier! Cesar has used a Westie as a spokesdog since the company began. In addition, the clothing brand Juicy Couture and White Whiskey both use Westies as their spokesdogs.

Some dogs don't have individual hot spots, but the allergy shows up on their entire coat. If your Westie seems to be shedding more fur than normal, take him to the vet to be checked for food allergies.

If you give your dog something his stomach cannot handle, it will probably be obvious when your dog is unable to hold his bowels. If he is already house trained, he will probably either pant at you or whimper to let you know he needs to go outside. Get him outside as quickly as you can so that he does not have an accident. Flatulence will also probably occur more often if your Westie has a food intolerance.

Since the symptoms of food allergies and intolerances look similar to a reaction to nutritional deficiencies, you should visit your vet immediately! This is especially true if you notice any problems with your dog's coat or skin.

CHAPTER 14
Playtime and Exercise

Though Westies are energetic dogs, they are medium-sized, so tiring them out will be a lot easier than a large, high-energy dog. Still, when you have a high energy, intelligent canine, you have to make sure that you keep that energy pretty much burned off so that your dog doesn't decide to entertain himself at the expense of your home, furniture, and hearing—your Westie may bark when bored. Here are the primary benefits of ensuring your Westie gets adequate activity every day:

- It helps keep your dog at a healthier weight.
- He will be tired enough not to be too much trouble, especially if you need to leave him alone for a little while.
- Exercise is a great time to bond with your Westie.

Photo Courtesy of Cheryl Kellar

Exercise Needs

"A Westie is an active dog and enjoys outside activities, such as swimming, running, and chasing. They have a very muscular build as a whole, so they need to be kept fit with some type of daily exercise, even if it is just running around and playing outside."

MELANIE CLARK
Gap Kennels

Westies need approximately an hour of vigorous daily exercise until they reach their senior years (Chapter 18). Aim for a 30-minute vigorous walk or jog in the morning and another 30-minute round of activities in the evening. If your Westie shows a tendency to be a bit mellower, you can adjust the exercise schedule. However, it is best to ensure that even calmer Westies get at least 30 minutes of real exercise daily.

If your Westie is not getting enough activity, it will probably be very obvious. They tend to be prolific diggers, and this is something they will do with great aplomb if they have excess energy. If they are trapped inside, they can be very destructive, including chewing on furniture, running into things, and digging up your carpet. Alternatively, your bored Westie could escape or become aggressive.

Since walks and jogs do get tiring—there will be days when it is rainy, too cold, too hot, or you just don't feel like leaving home—there are plenty of activities that can help you tire out your pup without leaving home.

Outdoor Activities

Given the breed's centuries of being outdoor dogs, your Westie is nearly guaranteed to enjoy outdoor activities. There are a lot of things you can do with him that will keep you both very entertained.

Doggie Soccer

If you or someone in your family loves soccer, your Westie could be an ideal partner for the sport. Make sure to teach your Westie all of the basic commands (Chapter 12) before beginning this activity. Teaching a dog to play soccer is tricky and requires a good bit of patience. However, once a

Westie knows how to play, it can be a lot of fun. After all, your dog already loves to chase, so it's just a matter of teaching him how to handle the ball.

Your Westie will very likely hog the ball in the beginning, even though he can't grip it with his teeth. You will need to show him how to nudge the ball and share it, which you can do by having two or more people play together as a demonstration. Watch YouTube clips for different ideas for how to get the general idea across to your Westie.

In the beginning, you'll have to play without lines as your Westie gets used to running around and sharing the ball. Once your Westie is adept at moving the ball around, you can start to introduce the lines. Once he understands not to knock the ball outside of the lines, you can get together a couple of teams and let your Westie be a member of your team. It is very likely that you will be tired long before your pup is ready to stop playing.

Be careful about playing on hot days as you don't want your Westie to get too hot. They aren't prone to overheating, but they don't have the ability to sweat like humans, so be aware of when your Westie needs to stop—odds are he won't stop if you don't.

Photo Courtesy
of Jolyn Zimmermann

Agility Training and Casual Courses

Better known as obstacle courses, agility training is a great way to keep your adult dog running and happy. You get to guide your dog through the course, helping not only to build your bond but also to give your dog a chance to feel more comfortable when he is outside the home, or at least learn that he doesn't need to try to dominate everyone in the area. Since you are the one in control, your dog will likely be confused in the beginning, so be prepared to look a bit silly at first. The point is to have fun and to keep your dog engaged, so getting and keeping his attention is key to being successful.

FUN FACT
Prey Drive?

West Highland White Terriers have a strong prey drive, most likely because they were initially bred to hunt rodents. A high prey drive may mean that these dogs are incompatible with cats, but some can adjust to cats in the home. Becoming comfortable with cats may be easier if the puppy is raised with cats. A high prey drive can make a well-fitting harness extra important on walks where squirrels, rabbits, or other small game may be nearby and available to chase.

Two to three hours of dedicated time a week are recommended for training your Westie, with one of those hours going to a weekly class that teaches him all of the complex commands that he needs to know for an agility course. The more you can train at home, the better your dog will do in this sport.

You can also create your own course at home, giving your Westie a series of over, under, and around sections to really keep him moving. A great way to ensure your dog gets the necessary activity on days when going outside just isn't something you want to do is to assemble structures of chairs, blankets, and other things your dog can easily crawl under.

Tricks – for Fun!

If your Westie enjoys training, tricks are a form of exercise he might like. It's a fantastic way to bond and tire your dog out with minimal exertion on your part. The best way to get ideas for tricks your dog can do is to go online and look for videos. Once your dog reliably responds to all the commands in Chapter 12, you can start teaching him to do things like roll over, dance, and play dead.

Great Walking Companion

As long as it isn't too hot or too cold outside, a nice 20- to 30-minute walk around the neighborhood two or three times a day is the perfect daily exercise for you and your dog. Your Westie will likely be bouncy and proud or curious and excited as you stroll around the blocks. If there is a nearby park, this will be a great place to go. It isn't likely that your dog will need a frequent change of venue for the walks, making it easier to walk with your pup on a regular basis.

His Own Digging Space

Instead of trying to have your Westie fight a natural desire to dig, play into it and create a digging space just for him. Given that your dog is probably going to start digging if given a couple of seconds alone, having a dedicated space lets your canine really enjoy the outdoors without destroying your yard.

To create your Westie's space, add sand or mulch to an area away from fences or the borders of your home and let your dog do what he loves to do. To encourage your dog to play just in that spot, bury toys, then watch him find them. This will be both mentally stimulating and physically tiring for your Westie, so end the game with a nice belly rub session and a bit of peace and quiet.

If it is a rainy or cold day, you can always set up a little pillow fort inside and hide the toy in that. Your dog will have an absolute blast "digging," and you will likely have a great time heartily laughing at the enthusiastic display.

Dog Parks

Since there are fantastic odds that your Westie is going to be sociable, taking time a couple of days a week to head to a dog park will mean other dogs can tire your pupper out. Give him about 30 minutes of playtime, and he'll probably be more than ready to go home. During the summer, plan to go in the early to middle of the morning. Dog parks are a great way to socialize your dog, though you will need to be careful in the early days to make sure your dog enjoys the playtime. Note that if your dog doesn't seem particularly happy being with other dogs, this may not be the best way to spend time outside the home.

Indoor Activities

If your Westie is a homebody, you'll definitely want options to entertain him. You'll also need plenty of options for rainy, hot, and colder weather.

Ball Herding

Since Westies are used to dealing with other animals, you can use that instinct for something incredibly entertaining—ball herding. Take a lot of larger balls, preferably balls that are softer but won't pop, and throw them in different directions, then have your Westie herd them into one area. This game will be easier if you have already trained your dog to play soccer.

Create a space on the floor, whether with sturdy pillows or chalk (if you are outside). Show your Westie that this is the space where the balls need to be herded, something you can do by having someone else "herd" the balls with you.

(1) Have your Westie sit in one place and watch you. You, your Westie, and the flock should all be within the outlined area in the beginning. Show your dog the flock of balls. You will need to get your dog to remain still when you "release" the flock. Focus on getting your Westie to sit still after you throw one ball. Over time, he will learn to wait as you release a greater number of balls.

(2) Gently roll one or two balls outside of the space, and have your Westie fetch them. If your Westie plays soccer, he will know how to nudge the balls back into the space a lot easier. Make sure to let your dog know that the space is the "pen" so that he will understand directions for the next couple of steps.

(3) When your dog understands that the flock belongs in the pen (this will probably take a couple of games for your Westie to really get the idea), you can finally start with the flock outside of the pen. Have your Westie nudge the herd into the pen. With each ball that he gets in the pen, give him a treat and a lot of praise. Once all of the balls are penned, be incredibly enthusiastic, praising your dog as Westies are not used to "herding" inanimate objects, making this not exactly a natural game.

(4) When your dog gets adept at the game, start timing him. Make sure that your expectations are realistic based on the length of time it takes your dog to recover the balls. How long you give your pupper will likely depend on how many balls you use. This is a game that should be customized to your dog and his abilities. If you start to see frustration in

141

Photo Courtesy of Tanya Lawson

your dog, give him more time to complete the task. For example, give him a minute per ball if you have the ball only a couple of feet from the pen. If you start the balls further from the destination, give your dog more time for each ball. As he gets better, you can start reducing the time to challenge your dog.

Puzzle Toys!

Puzzle toys are a fun way to get your dog to move around without you having to do much. Most puzzle toys are food-based, so the dog will need to figure out how to get the treats out. If you use these toys, keep in mind that your dog isn't likely to work off the extra calories consumed from puzzle treats.

Social Media Darling

Westies are very photogenic. If you really want an activity for lazy days, create a social media account for your Westie and let him really ham it up for the camera. Just make sure you don't make your dog uncomfortable. Your Westie may not be interested in wearing costumes or doing particular activities. Don't force your dog to do things he doesn't like, and definitely do not put him in any danger. You should both have a great time with his social media account. One of the best things about this activity is that your dog won't age out of being a social media darling.

What to Avoid

There are a lot of things you can do to exercise a Westie, but with an intelligent dog like this, you have to be very careful about not letting him get into trouble. The following are things you should avoid.

Leaving Him Alone Outside

Because your Westie is a medium-sized dog, you don't have to worry about him being snatched by a bird of prey, but that doesn't mean he is safe while alone outdoors. Westies have been chasing and digging for centuries, and your fence isn't going to stop your little friend. When it's time for a potty break, always go with your dog.

Yes, putting your dog out in the backyard alone is easier, especially if you are running late for work or it's snowing or raining. But the time you save is negated if your dog manages to get out of your yard because you weren't watching him. Never put your dog outside and hope that he will get his daily exercise. It's an activity that requires both of you—especially since your bored Westie will learn that getting out of the yard will get him more attention as you try to chase him.

Off Leash

Unless you are at a dog park or in a fenced-in location, don't take your Westie off the leash. He may start chasing an animal and get lost or hurt. Trying to call out to your Westie to get him to stop is not likely to be effective when he is running away because he will expect you to chase behind him—that's how a Westie's breeding works. He takes off, and his people follow him. For safety's sake, just keep him on the leash.

CHAPTER 15
Grooming – Productive Bonding

Despite their longer coats, Westies aren't prolific shedders. But it is recommended that you brush your Westie every day to keep his fur from getting dirty and matted. Fortunately, this can be a pretty enjoyable experience for both of you. That said, you may want to make sure your Westie is tired out before you get started grooming.

Photo Courtesy of Michael and Jennifer Luciano

In addition, there are other regular grooming tasks you will need to do, including taking care of your Westie's teeth and toenails. This could be tricky given that your dog isn't likely to want to sit still for either of these activities.

Your Westie could have one of a few skin conditions (Chapter 17). By grooming him every day, you can make sure to take care of his skin and keep it from getting irritated. It also means that you need to be careful when you brush him so that you don't hurt him.

Grooming Tools

"A metal comb (called a Greyhound comb) is perfect for getting out dead hair and tangles. Brushes are good for smoothing, but dead hair needs to be removed (stripped) and a brush will not do it. Dead hair itches, and the Westie will start biting it to get it out. Then, the biting can cause a hole in the coat and a sore spot."

MARLEEN C BURFORD
MARDOT

When it comes to their coats, Westies are unique; they have both hair and fur. That means taking care of your dog's coat will be a bit different from most other breeds. The good news is that you aren't going to need a whole lot of tools to groom your pup. The bad news is that every Westie has a different kind of coat, so that could mean trial and error until you find the right grooming tools for your dog. Instead of specific brush types, it's best to look for a few characteristics.

- The brush should have durable pins that don't recess after only a couple of uses.

- Make sure that the brush pins have comfortable tips; they shouldn't scratch your dog's skin. With their double coats, pinheads can irritate the skin as you try to work out the tangles and snarls.

- Get a brush that fits easily in your hand so that you have more control with each stroke.

- Slicker brushes are great for managing the topcoat, especially if it is particularly thick. For thinner topcoats, slicker brushes could be a bit uncomfortable for your Westie.

- Besides the brush, you will need to get a few other tools to properly take care of your pup.

- Shampoo (Make sure you use dog shampoo, not human, and check Bark Space for the latest recommendations.)
- Nail trimmers
- Toothbrush and dog toothpaste (not human—it's toxic for dogs!). (Check the American Kennel Club for the latest recommendations for the Westie, as they tend to have dental problems.)

Coat Management

"Decide what kind of fur you like. If you want stiffer fur, you'll want to have your dog stripped. If you like the softer fur, you'll want to have your pooch clipped. However, if you're okay with a lot of brushing, and you're not in a super hot climate, there's also nothing wrong with letting them go au naturel!"

FRANCES ROBERSON
Nancy's Westies

Always make sure to tire your dog before you start brushing. You cannot rush the process. To get all of the tangles and other issues taken care of, you are going to need a good bit of time, so you need your dog to sit still for a while. You'll know when you don't need to dedicate time to tiring your dog when he starts to slow down as a senior or shows an interest in just sitting and letting you pet and brush him.

Puppies

The difficulty when grooming a puppy is fairly universal because puppies are notorious for squirming! A daily brushing is the best way to both reduce how much your puppy sheds and to bond with your dog. Yes, it will be a bit challenging in the beginning because puppies don't sit still for prolonged periods of time; there will be a lot of wiggling and attempts to play. Trying to tell your puppy that the brush is not a toy clearly won't work, so be patient during each brushing session!

On the other hand, your pup will be so adorable that you probably won't mind a grooming session taking a bit longer than expected. Just make sure you let your pup know grooming is serious business, and playing comes after grooming. Otherwise, your Westie is going to always try to play, which will make brushing him more time-consuming.

Try planning to brush your puppy after a vigorous exercise session. If you find your puppy has trouble sitting still, you can make brushing sessions shorter but do it more than once a day until he gets used to the routine.

Adult Dogs

Brushing needs to be daily for the adults, especially after a lot of outdoor activity. Whatever brush you find works for your dog, the brushings should be both relaxing to your pup and beneficial for his skin. The grooming process stimulates the skin to release oils that make the fur shinier and more resistant to dirt, and this is absolutely necessary for Westies. If you regularly brush your dog, it can help reduce how often you have to bathe your Westie.

Brushing your dog is about more than just removing excess fur and improving the coat's shine. You need to spend each grooming session looking for skin problems, lumps, flea or tick bites, and other problems when you brush your buddy. Bushing reveals potential issues that you should monitor, and if symptoms become severe, you should have them checked out at the vet.

If you rescued an adult Westie, it might take a little while to get the dog used to being brushed frequently. If your dog does not feel comfortable in the beginning when you brush his fur, work the routine into your schedule, just like training, so he will get accustomed to the task.

Senior Dogs

You can brush your senior dog more often if you would like, as the extra affection and time you give him will likely be welcome. After all, he's slowing down, and just relaxing with you will be enjoyable for him (and the warmth of your hands will feel really good on his aging body). Grooming sessions are an appropriate time to check for problems while giving your older pup a nice massage to ease any pain. Look for any changes to the skin, such as bumps or fatty lumps. These may need to be mentioned to the vet during a regular visit.

Allergies

Some Westies have skin allergies. If your Westie is suffering from hot spots, or if you notice his coat is thinning, then you should look for the following allergic reactions:

- Wounds take longer to heal
- Weak immune system
- Aching joints
- Hair is falling out
- Ear infections

Regular brushing keeps you aware of the health of your Westie's coat. This will help you identify when your little dear is suffering from allergies so you can take him to the vet immediately.

Bath Time

"A Westie should not be bathed more than once a month and always use a moisturizing shampoo. Excessive washing can cause your Westie to have dry skin; therefore, affecting the natural balance in your Westie's coat. You can always rinse your Westie off with water in between baths, or just bath the area that is most dirty. If your Westie gets muddy (which is one of their favorite things to do), just let it dry and then brush it out. Your Westie will stay much cleaner than you would think."

MELANIE CLARK
Gap Kennels

Since regular brushing helps stimulate the natural oils of the breed, most Westie people recommend just bathing as needed. If you prefer to be able to set a schedule, once a quarter (once every three months) or twice a year will probably keep your Westie from getting stinky. If your Westie gets muddy or really dirty, make sure to bathe him so that the dirt and mud don't get trapped in the fur. Avoid bathing him too often, though, since it can irritate your dog's skin and remove necessary oils in his fur.

Photo Courtesy of Lee Russell

Whenever you go exploring or hiking with your Westie, most likely you will need to bathe your canine after each adventure. Make sure the water isn't too cold or too hot but comfortably warm, and always avoid getting his head wet. How to wash your dog's face is covered in the next section.

1. Gather everything you will need before you start your dog's bath. At a minimum, you need the following:
   a. shampoo and conditioners made specifically for dogs,
   b. cup for pouring water (if bathing in a tub),
   c. towels,
   d. brushes for after the drying process,
   e. non-slip tub mat if you use a tub, and
   f. buckets and a hose to rinse off if you bathe your dog outside.

2. Take your Westie out for a walk. This will tire your dog and make him a little hotter and less fearful—he might even appreciate the bath's cooling effect.

3. Run the water, making sure the temperature is lukewarm but not hot, especially if you have just finished a walk. If you are washing your Westie in a bathtub, you only need enough water to cover your pup's stomach. Do not fully cover your dog's body.

4. Pick up your dog if you are using a bathtub, and talk in a strong, confident voice.

(5) Place the dog in the tub and use the cup to wash the dog. Don't use too much soap—it isn't necessary. You can fully soak the dog, starting at the neck and going to the rump. It is fine to get him wet and to suds him up all at once, or you can do it a little at a time if your dog is very wiggly. Just make sure you don't get any water on his head.

(6) Confidently talk to your Westie while you are bathing him.

(7) Make sure you don't pour water on your dog's head or in his eyes or ears. Use a wet hand and gently scrub. (Follow the steps in the next section for how to carefully wash your dog's face and ears.)

(8) When you rinse, make sure to brush up against the fur so that there is no shampoo left.

(9) Take your Westie out of the water and towel him dry.

(10) Make sure to give special attention to drying around the head and face.

(11) Brush your dog when you are finished.

(12) Give him a treat if he was particularly upset about the bath.

You can use these practices with other kinds of bathing, such as outside or at a public washing facility; modify them as necessary.

The first few times you bathe your dog, pay attention to the things that bother or scare your Westie. If he is afraid of running water, make sure you don't have the water running when your dog is in the tub. If he moves around a lot when you start to apply the shampoo, it could indicate the smell is too strong. Modify the process as necessary in order to make it as comfortable for your dog as possible.

FUN FACT
What Is Hand Stripping?

Hand stripping is the grooming process of removing your Westie's guard hairs by plucking. A puppy's coat can first be stripped at 16 weeks, and this should be done approximately every eight weeks. Stripping a Westie's coat is used to achieve the ideal coat texture outlined by the breed standard and should not be painful for your dog if done correctly. As always, consult with your groomer or veterinarian when deciding if this process is suitable for your dog.

Keep a calm, loving tone as you wash your dog to make the process a little easier next time. Sure, your Westie may whine, throw a tantrum, or wiggle excessively, but a calm reaction will teach your dog that bathing is a necessary part of being a member of the pack.

Cleaning Eyes and Ears

When bathing your dog, use a washcloth to wash his face and ears, and ALWAYS avoid getting water in his ears, which can lead to problems.

You will need to make weekly checks around your Westie's eyes and ears to detect infections early. The following are signs of a problem:

- Frequent head shaking or tilting
- Regular scratching at ears
- Swollen or red ears
- A smell or discharge from the ears

Photo Courtesy of Aubrey Santillo

If you notice any problems with your Westie's ears, make an appointment with your vet. Never try to treat an infection on your own; hydrogen peroxide, cotton swabs, and other cleaning tools should never be used in a dog's ears. Your vet can show you how to clean your dog's ears correctly.

Westies have a few genetic eye and ear conditions (See Chapter 17), so take time to always check your dog's eyes while you are grooming him.

Cataracts are a fairly common problem for all dogs as they age. If you see cloudy eyes, have your Westie checked.

Trimming Nails

Cutting a Westie's nails can be difficult because dogs can be sensitive about someone touching their paws. Odds are your dog will have dark nails, which makes it difficult to cut them to the correct length without accidentally cutting the quick, the most sensitive part of the nail. It's best to have an expert cut your dog's nails until you understand how nail trimming is done. If you have never cut a dog's nails, ask a professional, like a groomer or a vet, to teach you the steps involved because nails can bleed a lot if they are not cut properly. If you know how to trim a dog's nails, make sure to have some styptic powder nearby in case you cut the nail too close.

If you want to trim your dog's nails yourself, there are nail grinders that can help lessen your worry about cutting the quick, but you will need to make sure you don't grind too much off the nail. Seek help from a professional before using the grinder, keep your dog calm during the process, and always think of your dog's safety first.

To know when your pup needs his nails cut, listen for clicking sounds on hard surfaces when your dog is walking. Those sounds indicate you should trim your dog's nails on a more frequent basis. As a general rule, once a month is recommended.

Dogs' nails have a small vein that runs through them, and for dogs with white nails, you can see the pink vein. If your dog has black nails, never try to cut his nails without getting professional assistance a few times because you cannot see where that vein ends, and you will need to learn to avoid cutting the nail too much.

Once you are comfortable cutting your dog's nails, you will need a set of nail clippers for small to medium-sized dog paws (depending on the size of your Westie).

1. Take your dog's paw gently and firmly. If your dog squirms, you may need to tire out your dog before trying to cut his nails.

2. Push any hair away from the nail you want to cut.

3. Look for the pink vein (if your dog has light-colored nails), then be mindful of it as you prepare to cut the first nail.

4. Position the nail clipper where the nail begins to curve, making sure the vein is not going to be cut.

5. Check the under part of the nail to see if you can see a pinkish-gray area. If you can see it, do not cut any further. If you don't see it and you want to cut a little more, repeat step four.

You will need to repeat this process for every nail on all four paws.

* If your dog's nail starts to bleed, apply styptic powder or silver nitrate sticks (the sticks are less messy) to the area. Follow the directions on the container to help stem the flow. Continue to hold your dog's paw until it stops bleeding before you let go of your dog. You can use hydrogen peroxide to clean up the blood on the fur after the nail stops bleeding.

If you only cut a little each time, you will need to cut your dog's nails once a month. If you cut a little further, you may be able to cut his nails just once a quarter.

Oral Health

Since Westies tend to have dental issues, it is best to be extra careful with your Westie's oral hygiene. Besides healthy food, there are two recommendations to take care of your Westie's teeth.

1. Brush your Westie's teeth twice a week.
2. Give your Westie dental chew treats.

Brushing Your Dog's Teeth

You have to learn to be patient and keep teeth cleaning from being an all-out fight with your dog. Brushing a dog's teeth is a little weird, and your Westie may not be terribly happy with someone putting stuff in his mouth. However, once he is accustomed to it, the task will likely only take a few minutes a day. Regular brushing keeps down plaque and tartar, making your pup's teeth healthier.

Always use a toothpaste that is made for dogs; human toothpaste can be toxic for your little friend. There are assorted flavors of dog toothpaste, which will make it easier when brushing your Westie's teeth, and it could also be entertaining as he tries to eat the meat-flavored toothpaste!

THE FOLLOWING ARE THE STEPS FOR BRUSHING YOUR DOG'S TEETH:

1. Put a little toothpaste on your finger and hold it out to your dog.
2. Let your dog lick the toothpaste from your finger.
3. Praise your dog for trying something new.
4. Put a little toothpaste on your finger again, lift your dog's upper lip, and begin to rub in circles along your Westie's gums. Your pup will likely make it difficult by constantly trying to lick your finger. Give your puppy praise when he doesn't lick the toothpaste or doesn't wiggle too much.
   a. Try to move your finger in a circular motion. This will be very tricky, especially if you have a puppy with sharp baby teeth.
   b. Try to keep the dog still without putting him in a vise. As your puppy gets bigger, he'll need to know how to sit for the cleaning process voluntarily.
5. Try to massage both the top and bottom gums. It is likely the first few times you won't be able to do much more than get your finger in your dog's mouth, and that's okay. Over time, your dog will learn to listen because general behavioral training will reinforce listening to your commands.

155

(6) Stay positive. No, you probably won't be able to clean your dog's teeth properly for a while, and that is perfectly fine—as long as you keep working at it patiently and consistently.

Once your dog seems comfortable with having his teeth brushed with your finger, try the same steps with a canine toothbrush. (It could take a couple of weeks before you can graduate to this stage.)

Dental Chews

One of the healthiest treats to give any dog is dental chews. While you will need to keep count of the treats as a part of your dog's daily caloric intake, they help with taking care of your dog's teeth. They aren't a replacement for regular brushing, but they are a good complement. Dogs tend to love these treats, and they help improve your dog's breath, so it is a win-win. Make sure to do your research to ensure that you are giving your dog the healthiest dental chews. You don't want to give your Westie any treats that have questionable or uncertain ingredients.

CHAPTER 16
General Health Issues: Allergies, Parasites, and Vaccinations

Your Westie is nearly guaranteed to love going outside as it's a great place to play and chase small animals. Unfortunately, being outside comes with a lot of risks. Environmental factors largely determine whether or not your dog gets parasites. For example, if you live near a wooded area, your dog is at a greater risk of having ticks than a dog that lives in the city. Fleas are a universal problem for all dogs because fleas can live in any grass, short or long. If you notice rashes or skin irritation, it could be an allergic reaction or symptoms of a parasite. Talk to your vet about all potential environmental risks and any skin conditions you notice when you groom your dog.

Photo Courtesy
of Angela Venn

The Role of Your Veterinarian

Scheduled veterinary visits, routine vaccinations, and regular checkups make for a healthy Westie. If your dog seems sluggish or less excited than usual, it could be a sign there is something wrong with him. Fortunately, the breed's personality tends to make it easy to tell when your dog isn't feeling well. Annual visits to the vet will help catch any problems that might be slowly draining the energy or the health from your dog.

Regular checkups also make sure that your Westie is aging well. If your dog shows symptoms of a potential problem, an early diagnosis will address the problem. You and your vet can create a plan to manage any pain or problems that come with your dog's aging process. The vet may recommend adjustments to your schedule to accommodate your pup's aging body and his diminishing abilities. This will ensure that you can keep having fun together without hurting your dog.

Vets can provide treatment or preventive medication for parasites and other microscopic threats that your dog might encounter on a daily basis, whether playing outside or when he is exposed to dogs or other animals.

Allergies

Dog allergies are usually a result of allergens (such as dust, mold, or pollen), which irritate the skin or nasal passages. Dogs often develop allergies when they are between one and five years old. Once they develop an allergy, canines never outgrow the problem.

The scientific name for environmental allergies is atopic dermatitis. However, it is difficult to know if the problem is environmental or if it is a food you are feeding your dog.

The following symptoms can be seen when either type of allergy is present:

- Itching/scratching, particularly around the face
- Hot spots
- Ear infections
- Skin infections
- Runny eyes and nose (not as common)

Since the symptoms are the same for food and environmental allergies, your vet will help determine the cause. If your dog has a food allergy, change the food that you give him. If he has an environmental allergy, he will need medication, just as humans do. There are several types of medications that can help your dog become less sensitive to allergens:

- **ANTIBACTERIAL/ANTIFUNGAL** – These treatments only address the problems that come with allergies; shampoos, pills, and creams usually do not directly treat the allergy itself.
- **ANTI-INFLAMMATORIES** – These are over-the-counter medications, which are comparable to allergy medicine for people. Don't give your dog any medication without first consulting with the vet. You will need to monitor your dog to see if he has any adverse effects. If your dog is lethargic, has diarrhea, or shows signs of dehydration, consult with your vet immediately.
- **IMMUNOTHERAPY** – This is a series of shots that can help reduce your dog's sensitivity to whatever he is allergic to. You can learn from your vet how to give your dog these shots at home. Scientists are also developing an oral version of this medication to make it easier to take care of your dog.
- **TOPICAL** – This medication tends to be a type of shampoo and conditioner that will remove any allergens from your dog's fur. Giving your dog a warm (not hot) bath can also help relieve itching.

To determine the best treatment for your situation, talk with your vet.

Inhalant and Environmental Allergies

Inhalant allergies are caused by things like dust, pollen, mold, and dog dander. Your dog might scratch at a particular hotspot, or he might paw at his eyes and ears. Some dogs have runny noses and sneeze prolifically, in addition to scratching.

Contact Allergies

Contact allergies mean that your dog has touched something that triggers an allergic reaction. Things like wool, chemicals in a flea treatment, and certain grasses can trigger irritation in a dog's skin, even causing discoloration. If left untreated, the allergic reaction can cause the affected area to emit a strong odor or cause fur loss.

Like food allergies, contact allergies are easy to treat because once you know what is irritating your dog's skin, you can remove the problem.

Fleas and Ticks

Make it a habit to check for ticks after every outing into the woods or near long grass or wild plants. Comb through your dog's fur and check his skin for signs of irritation and for any parasites. Since you will be doing this several times a week, you should be able to recognize when there's a change, such as a new bump.

Fleas are problematic because they're far more mobile than ticks. The best way to look for fleas is to make it a regular part of your brushing sessions. If you see black specks on the flea comb after brushing through your dog's fur, this could be a sign of fleas.

HELPFUL TIP

Identifying Dry Eyes

Westies can be prone to developing a condition known as dry eyes or kerato-conjunctivitis sicca (KCS). Symptoms of this disease include red or irritated eyes, yellowish discharge, and excessive squinting. Diagnosis is made by a vet using the Shirmer tear test (STT), which measures the number of tears produced by your dog in one minute. Treatments aim to stimulate tear production and replace the protective tear film that shields your dog's cornea. Untreated KCS can lead to eye damage and blindness.

Instead of using a comb, you can also put your dog on a white towel and run your hand over the fur. Fleas and flea dirt are likely to fall onto the towel. Fleas often are seen on the stomach, so you may notice them when your pup wants a belly rub. You can also look for behavioral indicators, such as incessant scratching and licking. If fleas are a problem, you will need to use flea preventative products on a regular basis once your puppy has reached the appropriate age.

Both fleas and ticks can carry parasites and illnesses that can be passed on to you and your family. Ticks carry Lyme disease, which can be debilitating or deadly if untreated. Lyme disease symptoms include headaches, fever, and fatigue. The bite itself often has a red circle around it. Ticks will fall off your dog once they are full, so if you find a tick on your dog, it will either be looking for a place to latch onto your dog, or it will be feeding. Use the following steps to remove the tick if it has latched onto your dog.

(1) Apply rubbing alcohol to the area where the tick is located.

(2) Use tweezers to pull the tick off your dog. Do not use your fingers because infections are transmitted through blood, and you don't want the tick to latch onto you.

③ Place the tick in a bag and make sure it is secure so that it does not fall out. The vet can assess the type of tick for diagnostic purposes since different types of ticks carry different diseases.

④ Examine the spot where the tick was to make sure it is fully removed. Sometimes the head will remain under the dog's skin, so make sure all of the tick has been removed.

⑤ Set up a meeting with the vet to have your dog checked.

The FDA has issued a warning about some store-bought treatments for fleas and ticks. Treatments can be applied monthly, or you can purchase a collar for constant protection. Either way, make sure the treatment does not contain isoxazoline, which can have a negative effect on some pets. (This chemical is found in Bravecto, Nexgard, Credelio, and Simparica.)

Most ingredients in these treatments are safe if the proper dose is used. However, if you use a product that is meant for a larger dog, the effects can be toxic to your smaller dog. Consult your vet for recommended treatments and administer the appropriate dose of flea and tick repellant for your dog's size and needs. When you start applying the treatment, watch your dog for the following issues:

- Diarrhea/vomiting
- Trembling
- Lethargy
- Seizures

Photo Courtesy of Ellie Standidge

Take your dog to the vet if you notice any of these issues.

Never use any cat product on a dog and vice versa. If your dog is sick, pregnant, or nursing, you may need to look for an alternative preventative treatment. If you have a cat or young children, you should choose one of the other preventative options for keeping fleas and ticks away. This is because flea collars contain an ingredient that is lethal to felines and which might be carcinogenic to humans.

The packaging on flea treatments will advise you when to begin treating your dog based on his current age and size. Different brands have different recommendations, and you don't want to start treating your puppy too early. There are also important steps to applying the treatment. Make sure you understand all of the steps before purchasing the flea treatment.

If you want to use natural products instead of chemicals, research the alternatives and decide what works best for your Westie. Verify that any natural products work before you buy them, and make sure you consult with your vet. Establish a regular monthly schedule and add it to your calendar so that you remember to consistently treat your dog for fleas and ticks.

Parasitic Worms

Although worms are a less common problem than fleas and ticks, they can be far more dangerous. The following lists the types of worms that you should be aware of:

- Heartworms
- Hookworms
- Roundworms
- Tapeworms
- Whipworms

Unfortunately, there isn't an easy-to-recognize set of symptoms to help identify when your dog has worms. However, you can keep an eye out for the following symptoms, and if your dog shows any of these warning signs, schedule a visit to the vet:

- Your Westie is unexpectedly lethargic for a few days.
- Patches of fur begin to fall out (this will be noticeable if you brush your Westie regularly), or you notice patchy spaces in your dog's coat.
- Your dog's stomach becomes distended (expands) and looks like a potbelly.
- Your Westie begins coughing, vomiting, has diarrhea, or has a loss of appetite.

If you aren't sure about any symptom, it's always best to get your dog to the vet as soon as possible.

Heartworms

Heartworms are a significant threat to your dog's health and can be deadly as they can both slow and stop blood flow. As such, you should consistently treat your dog with heartworm protection.

Fortunately, there are medications that prevent your dog from developing heartworms. To prevent this deadly problem, you can give your dog a chewable medication, topical medicine, or you can request shots.

The heartworm parasite is carried by mosquitoes, which are nearly impossible to avoid in most regions of the country, and it is a condition that is costly and time-consuming to treat. The following are the steps involved in treating your dog for heartworms:

- The vet will draw blood for testing, which can cost as much as $1,000.
- Treatment will begin with some initial medications, including antibiotics and anti-inflammatory drugs.
- Following a month of the initial medication, your vet will give your dog three shots over the course of two months.

From the time of diagnosis until the confirmation your dog is free of heartworms, you will need to be extremely cautious when you exercise your dog because the worms are in your dog's heart, and that inhibits blood flow. This means raising your dog's heart rate too much could kill him. Your vet will tell you how best to exercise your canine during this time. Considering your Westie may be energetic, this could be a very rough time for both you and your dog.

Photo Courtesy of the Grimsley Family

Treatment will continue after the shots are complete. After approximately six months, your vet will conduct another blood test to ensure the worms are gone.

Once your dog is cleared of the parasites, you will need to begin medicating your dog against heartworms in the future. There will be lasting damage to your dog's heart, so you will need to ensure that your dog does not over exercise.

Intestinal Worms: Hookworms, Roundworms, Tapeworms, and Whipworms

All four of these worms thrive in your dog's intestinal tract, and they get there when your dog eats something contaminated. The following are the most common ways dogs ingest worms:

- Feces
- Small hosts, such as fleas, cockroaches, earthworms, and rodents
- Soil, including licking it from their fur and paws
- Contaminated water
- Mother's milk (If the mother has worms, she can pass them on to young puppies when they nurse.)

The following are the most common symptoms and problems caused by intestinal parasites:

- Anemia
- Blood loss
- Coughing
- Dehydration
- Diarrhea
- Large intestine inflammation
- Weight loss
- A pot-bellied appearance

If a dog lies in soil with hookworm larvae, the parasites can burrow through the canine's skin. Vets will conduct a diagnostic test to determine if your dog has this parasite, and if your dog does have hookworms, the vet will prescribe a dewormer. If your dog is infested with hookworms, you should visit a doctor yourself because humans can get hookworms, too. Being treated at the same time as your Westie will help stop the vicious cycle of continually trading off which of you has worms.

ROUNDWORMS are quite common, and at some point in their lives, most dogs have to be treated for them. The parasites primarily eat the digested food in your dog's stomach, getting the nutrients your dog needs. It is possible for larvae to remain in your dog's stomach even after all of the adult worms have been eradicated. If your Westie is pregnant, her puppies should be checked periodically to make sure the inactive larvae are not passed on to the puppies. The mother will also need to go through the same testing to make sure the worms don't make her sick.

TAPEWORMS are usually eaten when they are eggs and are carried by fleas or from the feces of other animals who also have tapeworms. The eggs develop in the canine's small intestine until they reach the adult stage. Over time, parts of the tapeworm will break off and can be seen in your dog's waste. If this happens, you should be very thorough when cleaning up any waste so other animals will not also contract tapeworms. While tapeworms are not usually fatal, they can cause weight loss and give your dog a potbelly. (The size of your dog's stomach depends on how big the worms grow in your dog's intestines.)

Your vet can test your dog for tapeworms and can prescribe medication to take care of the problem. The medication might include chewable tablets, regular tablets, or a powder that can be sprinkled on your dog's food. There is a minimal risk of humans catching tapeworms, but children are at the greatest risk. Be sure children wash their hands carefully when playing in areas used by your dog. It is also possible to contract tapeworms if a person swallows a flea, which is feasible if your dog and home have a serious infestation.

WHIPWORMS grow in the large intestine, and when in large numbers, they can be fatal. Their name is indicative of the appearance of their tails, which are thinner than their upper section. Like the other worms, you will need to have your dog tested to determine if he has acquired whipworms.

Staying current with flea treatments, properly disposing of your pet's waste, and making sure your Westie does not eat trash or animal waste will help prevent your dog from getting these parasites.

Medication to prevent these four parasites can often be included in your dog's heartworm medication. Be sure to speak with your vet regarding the different options.

Vaccinating Your Westie

Vaccination schedules are routine for most dog breeds, including Westies. Make sure to add this information to your calendar, and until your puppy has completed his vaccinations, he should avoid contact with other dogs.

The following list can help you schedule your Westie's vaccinations:

These shots protect your dog against a range of ailments. Keep in mind these shots should be a part of your dog's annual vet visit so you can continue to keep your pup safe!

Timeline	Shot		
6 to 8 weeks	Bordetella	Leptospira	DHPP – First shot
	Lyme	Influenza Virus-H3N8	Influenza Virus-H3N2
10 to 12 weeks	Leptospira	DHPP – Second shot	Rabies
	Lyme	Influenza Virus-H3N8	Influenza Virus-H3N2
14 to 16 weeks	DHPP – Third shot		
Annually	Leptospira	Bordetella	Rabies
	Lyme	Influenza Virus-H3N8	Influenza Virus-H3N2
Every 3 Years	DHPP Booster	Rabies (if opted for longer duration vaccination)	

Holistic Alternatives

Wanting to prevent exposure to chemical treatments for your dog makes sense, and there are many good reasons why people are moving to more holistic methods. However, if you decide to go with holistic medication, talk with your vet first about reputable options. You can also seek out Westie experts for recommendations before you start trying any holistic methods of care.

It is possible something like massage therapy can help your dog, especially as he ages. Even chiropractic therapy is available for dogs, but you will need to be sure to find a reputable chiropractor for your pup, so the treatment doesn't do more harm than good. Follow recommendations on reputable, holistic Westie websites to provide the best, safest care for your dog.

CHAPTER 17
Genetic Health Concerns Common to Westies

One of the biggest downsides about Westies is that there are a lot of potential health issues with the breed. A lot of this stems from the length of time the breed has been around and the way that breeding dogs has changed over the years—most older breeds have numerous serious issues, so it is not just Westies. Fortunately, most of the common problems are relatively minor, so it is more a matter of watching for problems that reduce quality of life than ones that pose a serious risk to your Westie's life. As the breed has an average life span between 12 and 14 years (though some Westies can live 16 years), you want to make sure you watch for potential problems to help your dog live a long, healthy life.

Common West Highland White Terrier Health Issues

You want to make sure that you catch health issues early to improve your dog's quality of life. Take the time to monitor your dog for those potential health problems.

Addison's Disease

Addison's disease can be a major health problem if your dog's adrenal gland is not producing enough of two hormones—aldosterone and cortisol. Aldosterone regulates your dog's electrolytes and hydration. Cortisol helps your dog deal with stress. Addison's disease can also destroy your dog's immune system, cause tumors to form, and increase the risk of cancer.

The following are symptoms of Addison's disease:

- Dehydration
- Depression
- Diarrhea
- Excessive thirst
- Lethargy
- Poor appetite
- Weakness
- Weight loss
- Vomiting

If you notice these symptoms, take your dog to the vet as soon as possible for a diagnosis. If your vet determines your dog has Addison's disease, oral medication is typically recommended, and it is possible your dog will need to be medicated for the rest of his life. Your vet will monitor your dog to decide if that is necessary. Once your dog starts feeling the effects of the medication, he should be able to resume normal meals and exercise.

Photo Courtesy of Margy van Gelder

Skin Conditions

Unfortunately, your Westie is likely to suffer from at least one skin condition as the breed's thicker two-layer coats can make them more sensitive. The good news is that it is fairly easy to take care of most of these skin conditions with daily careful grooming (Chapter 15).

ALLERGIES

Regular brushing ensures that you are more aware of the state of your Westie's coat, which can help you more quickly identify when your little dear is suffering from allergies. If you notice these issues, take your Westie to the vet. See Chapter 16 for detailed information on canine allergies.

CANINE SEBORRHEA

This is another condition that affects a dog's skin, and it can cause the skin to flake like dandruff. It can cause problems around your dog's ears, upper leg, elbows, ankles, and belly as it can begin to clump. The easiest way to spot signs that your dog has this condition is that he scratches the affected areas often and the areas have a distinctive, unpleasant odor. The incessant scratching can cause bleeding, secondary infection, and hair loss.

If you see that your dog has this (very treatable) condition, you'll need to get specialized shampoos and follow your vet's recommendations.

DRY SKIN

This isn't going to be too serious, but it can be pretty uncomfortable for your dog. And if he chews on dry areas, it can cause other problems. If you notice dandruff, take your dog to the vet. Usually, you will be given a special shampoo to use once or twice a week until the dry areas are healed.

HYPERPLASTIC DERMATOSIS

This is a skin condition that only appears in Westies, and it is incredibly rare (even in the breed). The symptoms are scaly, bumpy areas on the dog's skin, and if left untreated, it can become severe. At first, it will just look like a mild irritation, but it can get bad quickly.

This is a genetic issue, and it often doesn't present until a dog's skin is affected by other problems, like allergies or yeast infections. If you notice bumpy, scaly patches on your dog's skin, take him to the vet to be checked out. The condition is easily treated with an oral or topical medication.

*Photo Courtesy
of Ashley Mundadan*

Cushing's Disease

The scientific name of this disease is hyperadrenocorticism, and it occurs when the adrenal glands start to malfunction. As a result of this malfunction, your dog's body overproduces steroid hormones. The symptoms start to show early, but they are easy to miss because they appear to be minor issues.

Symptoms include your dog drinking more frequently and being hungrier than usual while being less active. These symptoms can be difficult to detect since you are less likely to notice them. However, as the problem progresses, your Westie may have a potbelly, develop thinner skin, and start to lose hair.

If your dog has Cushing's Disease, the vet will prescribe medication, and you will need to regularly monitor the condition. Initially, it will take close work with your vet to make sure the right dose of medication is determined.

Digestive Issues

It's fortunate that Westies tend to be picky eaters because they have a number of digestive issues, such as inflammatory bowel disease and pancreatitis. Problems usually cause pain and swelling of the dog's stomach. It's why it is also important to make sure your Westie does not eat things like animal feces and other random things off the ground that can upset his already sensitive digestive tract.

If your dog has digestive issues, tailoring his diet is usually the best way of dealing with the problems. Chapter 13 details the kinds of healthy diets that could help.

Orthopedic Diseases

Westies tend to have a number of orthopedic problems, especially as they age. The following are the primary joint problems your Westie may experience.

LUXATING PATELLA

Luxating patella is a kneecap disease that is common in Westies. This ailment is genetic, and your dog's kneecap may be dislocated.

If your dog has this problem, you may notice that he is skipping a step or limping on one leg. In more severe cases, your dog may not use the affected

Photo Courtesy
of Rachel Benecke

leg, meaning he hops around on three legs. When the kneecap slips back into place, your dog will resume a normal walk. As a dog ages, this problem will become worse as other issues present themselves, such as hip or elbow dysplasia or arthritis, all of which can impair your dog's ability to walk.

For more severe cases, vets can perform surgery. Most dogs will not require surgery, but you need to make sure that your dog does not overeat or become overweight, as this will make walking that much harder.

HIP AND ELBOW DYSPLASIA

Hip and elbow dysplasia are common ailments for medium- and larger-sized dogs. Their diet (Chapter 13) as a puppy can help minimize the problem when they are adults. Both types of dysplasia are a result of the dog's hip and leg sockets being malformed, which often leads to arthritis as the improper fit damages cartilage. The condition is possible to detect through X-rays by the time a dog becomes an adult.

This is a problem that your Westie may try to hide because he won't want to slow down. Your adult dog will walk a little more stiffly or may pant even when it's not hot. The condition usually becomes more obvious as a dog nears his golden years, and similar to the way older people tend to change their gait to accommodate pain, your dog may do the same. Getting up might be a little more difficult in the beginning and will likely get worse as he ages.

While surgery is an option in severe cases, most dogs can benefit from less invasive treatment:

- Anti-inflammatory medications – talk to your vet; (dogs should not have large doses of anti-inflammatory drugs on a daily basis the way people do since aspirin and anti-inflammatories can damage your dog's kidneys)
- Lower the amount of high-impact exercise your dog gets, especially on wood floors, tile, concrete, or other hard surfaces (given how much your dog probably loves to swim, you can move more to a swimming exercising regimen to keep them active without the jarring motions of walking and jogging on hard surfaces)
- Joint fluid modifiers
- Physical therapy
- Weight loss (for dogs who are overweight or obese)

HIPBONE ATROPHY

Also known as Legg-Calve-Perthes Disease, this is a rare condition that can cause bone loss around the top of the femur on a dog's back legs. This causes disintegration to the hips and other joints. It is unknown what causes it, but it starts to show when a dog is less than a year old. If you get a puppy from a breeder, you will need to watch for this. It is likely that you will be able to return the puppy as a part of the guarantee.

If you get an older dog, this problem will likely already be known, and you will be told about it when you adopt the dog. In this case, follow whatever recommendations you are given because it will likely follow a treatment that the dog has already been receiving. It is best not to adopt a Westie that has this particular problem if you aren't prepared to take care of a dog with a more serious disability. Such dogs really require specialized caregivers.

SWOLLEN JAW

The scientific name is craniomandibular osteopathy, and this is another more serious genetic problem. It presents with swelling of the jaw in young dogs, and it is typically obvious within the first year. It often isn't a problem in the long term as dogs can grow out of it.

If your puppy seems uncomfortable when opening his jaw to eat or bark or drools more than expected, take him to the vet to have him checked. It is likely the vet will take an X-ray of the skull to see if this is a problem.

Typically, treatment is just managing the pain until the dog outgrows the problem. Always follow the advice of your vet on what to give your dog—do not try to give your Westie the kinds of medicine people take because dogs do not process our medications very well.

Collie Eye Anomaly (CEA) and Colobomas

As the name suggests, this is a problem that is predominantly found in collies, but other breeds can have it, like Westies (though it is not common). It is a genetic mutation that can result in eyes that have many different defects. Often, it results in blindness, though it could just be different degrees of vision impairment. This is a disease that good breeders will screen for in their puppies when they are between six and eight weeks old. Sometimes it is more obvious in slightly older dogs, so vets should be looking for this in puppies over the first year of their life.

If your dog has this condition, your vet will recommend a full eye exam to determine the severity of the disease. This is more so you will know how to work with your dog because it cannot be cured. There are some surgical procedures that can be tried, but they are not guaranteed to fix the problem. Your dog has a better chance of getting better if the condition is caught when he is younger.

Pulmonary Fibrosis

HELPFUL TIP

Signs of Pulmonary Fibrosis

Westies may be prone to developing pulmonary fibrosis or lung scarring. The cause of this disease isn't widely understood, and the prognosis is a chronic, progressive disease. Signs that your dog may be suffering from this illness include blueish or pale gums, coughing, rapid breathing, and exercise intolerance. Diagnosis can only be made through testing such as chest X-rays.

Also known as Westie Lung Disease, this condition can result in scar tissue forming on the canine's lungs, and it can be fatal. Researchers and medical professionals don't know what causes the disease, but it is thought to be a result of long-term exposure to substances that can bother the dog's lungs, like allergens, smoke, and pollution.

Symptoms usually show in older dogs because it does take time to develop. Westies will start to show shortness of breath, are more easily exhausted, and have a reduction in energy.

There is no cure for this condition. The best thing that can be done is to make sure that you take care of your Westie over the course of his life, keeping him from being exposed to the kinds of things that hurt your lungs as well. Currently, there are no dedicated studies into the disease, but you should consult your vet as there are a few treatments that seem promising.

Shaker Dog Syndrome

This is a common problem among smaller dogs and is a neuromuscular ailment that causes tremors. Often symptoms begin around two years old and can result in seizures and problems with walking. The treatment is steroids, and sometimes this can be enough until the ailment goes away over time. There is no predictable amount of time for how long it will last, but some dogs will need steroids for the rest of their lives. Currently, there is no way to know which dogs will eventually be just fine and which ones will need help for years. The ailment is still being studied.

Common Owner Mistakes

"Do something as soon as you notice a problem. Westies are very stoic so it's hard to tell when they don't feel well. Have them blood tested, make sure to keep up on tooth care, and keep their feet clean. I bath our Westies with anti-bacterial-antifungal soap. Westies get fungus very easily which causes skin problems and ear problems."

MARLEEN C BURFORD
MARDOT

In addition to genetic problems, there are things you can do that could unintentionally damage your dog's health; these mistakes are related to diet and exercise levels. In the puppy stage, it is a difficult balance to strike as your puppy is curious and enthusiastic. Even when he is a fully grown dog, you have to make sure you are minimizing how much stress is placed on your Westie's body. Weight management is one important way of keeping your dog healthy. You need to balance your dog's diet with his level of activity to prevent exacerbation of hip and elbow dysplasia.

Failing to notice early signs of potential issues can be detrimental or even fatal to your Westie. Any changes in your Westie's behavior are likely a sign of something that should be checked by your vet.

Prevention and Monitoring

Checking your Westie's weight is important and should be done at least once a quarter or twice a year. You and your vet should keep an eye on your dog's weight as being overweight puts a strain on your dog's back, legs, joints, and muscles.

CHAPTER 18
The Aging West Highland White Terrier

Since the breed has a life span between 12 and 16 years, you will probably have a pretty good length of time with your adorable Westie. No matter how old your Westie is, it is never going to feel like you had enough time with your dog.

Westies are considered seniors when they are between seven and 10 years old. By the time your Westie reaches eight or nine, you will notice that your Westie doesn't have quite as much energy and will probably walk a little more stiffly than in previous years. A dog may remain healthy his whole life, but as the years start to take their toll, his body may not be able to enjoy the same activities.

The first signs of aging usually appear as stiffness in his gait or heavy panting that begins early in your walk. If you see these changes, start to cut back on the long walks and go for shorter ones more often. Your Westie may want to continue to be active, which calls for an adjustment in his activities but not a complete stop.

Be sure your pup doesn't overexert himself if he tries to remain active. Your Westie may not want to accept the fact that things are changing. Fortunately for your Westie, he will usually remain fairly happy as long as he is able to just lounge with you—it's one of the major benefits of having such an affable dog. He is always happy just being with his family, so he isn't going to be nearly so upset about losing his ability to be as active as many other breeds.

Another early symptom of aging in Westies is vision and hearing loss. The haze in your dog's eyes is a sign that his vision isn't quite what it used to be and could be a sign of cataracts. If you notice your dog being less aware of his surroundings, talk about this with your vet. Westies usually don't go completely blind or deaf, but you will want to know if his ability to see or hear is impaired.

There is a reason this period of time is called the golden years—you can relax and enjoy this time of your dog's life as well. You don't have to worry about him tearing up things because he's bored or becoming overexcited when seeing a squirrel during his walks. Instead, you can enjoy lazy evenings, peaceful weekends, and less strenuous exercise. It's easy to make the senior years incredibly enjoyable for your Westie and yourself by making the necessary adjustments.

Photo Courtesy of Cheryl Kellar

Senior Care Challenges – Common Physical Disorders Related to Aging

Accommodations you should make for your senior Westie include:

● Set water bowls in a couple of different places so that your dog can reach them easily.

● Cover hard floor surfaces (such as tile, hardwood, and vinyl) with non-slip carpets or rugs.

● Use cushions and softer bedding for your Westie to make things more comfortable. There are even bed warmers for dogs if your Westie displays achy joints or muscles. You also need to make sure he isn't too warm, so this can be a fine balancing act.

● To improve his circulation, increase how often you brush your Westie.

● Keep your dog inside in extreme heat or cold. An old canine cannot handle changes in temperature as well as he once did.

● Use stairs or ramps so that your old pup doesn't have to do any jumping.

● Avoid moving furniture around in your home, particularly if your Westie shows signs of problems with his eyesight or if he has dementia. A familiar home is more comforting and less stressful for your pet as he ages. If your Westie isn't able to see as clearly as he once did, you should make sure his surroundings remain familiar to him, which will make it easier for him to move around without hurting himself.

● Consider setting up an area for your dog that allows him to avoid stairs, especially if climbing seems to bother him.

● Create a space with fewer distractions and noises where your Westie can relax. Don't make your old friend feel isolated; instead, give him a place where he can get away from everyone if he needs to be alone.

● Be prepared to let your dog go outside for restroom breaks more often.

Previous chapters address illnesses that are common in a Westie. However, old age tends to bring a slew of ailments that are not particular to any one breed. Here are other things you will need to watch for (as well as talking to your vet about if they occur):

● Arthritis is probably the most common ailment in any dog breed, and the Westie is no exception. If your dog is experiencing stiffness and pain after normal activities, talk with your vet about ways to help minimize your Westie's discomfort.

- Gum disease is a common issue in older dogs as well, and you should continue brushing your dog's teeth on a regular basis as he ages. A regular check of your Westie's teeth and gums can help ensure no problem develops.

- Loss of eyesight or blindness is relatively common in older dogs, just as it is in humans. Have your dog's vision checked at least once a year or more often if it is obvious his eyesight is failing.

- Kidney disease is a frequent problem in older dogs and one that you should watch for as your Westie ages. If your canine drinks a lot of water and has accidents frequently, take him to the vet as soon as possible.

- Although diabetes is usually thought of as a genetic condition, any Westie can become diabetic if not fed and exercised properly.

Vet Visits – The Importance of Regular Vet Visits and What to Expect

As your Westie ages, slowing down and occasional pain will become obvious. If your Westie has a debilitating ailment or condition, discuss options for giving him a better quality of life. For example, wheelchairs are available if your Westie shows problems with mobility.

Just as humans visit the doctor more often as they age, you'll need to take your dog to see your vet with greater frequency, too. The vet can make sure your Westie stays active without overdoing it, and he can help alleviate unnecessary stress in your dog's life.

Based on your Westie's changing personality and physical abilities, your vet might recommend changes to your dog's daily schedule and to his typical activities to keep your Westie happy and active during the later years.

The following are the kinds of things to expect when you go to the vet:

- Your vet will talk about your dog's history even if you have visited every year. This conversation is necessary to see how your dog's life has changed over time and to pinpoint when problems manifested themselves or got worse.

- Your vet will probably conduct a complete physical examination to assess your dog's current health.

- Depending on your dog's age and on his health, your vet may want to run some tests. The following are some of the most common tests for older dogs:
  - Arthropod-borne disease testing, which involves drawing blood and testing it for viral infections
  - Chemistry screening for kidney, liver, and sugar evaluation
  - Complete blood count
  - Fecal flotation, which involves mixing your dog's poop with a special liquid to test for worms and other parasites
  - Heartworm testing
  - Urinalysis, which tests your dog's urine to check the health of his kidneys and urinary system
  - Routine wellness check, which the vet has been conducting on your dog for years
  - Any breed-specific tests for your aging Westie.

Changes That Might Occur

"As Westies age they tend to become calmer, but also don't like new things. So if an older Westie is not familiar with small children, but suddenly is around a small, loud, fast moving child this could cause the Westie to become protective and aggressive. This is why socialization is so important and you should always introduce Westies to children in their younger years."

LEA LESLIE
Westiesworldforever

Keep an eye out for different signs that your dog is slowing down. This will help you to know when to adjust the setup around your home and to reduce how much your old pup is exercising.

Appetite and Nutritional Requirements

With less exercise, your dog won't need as many calories as usual, which means you will need to adjust his diet. If you opted to feed your Westie commercial dog food, make sure to switch to a senior dog formula. Senior food

is designed for the changing dietary needs of older dogs by including fewer calories and adding more nutrients.

If you prepare dog food at home, talk to your vet and research how best to reduce calories without sacrificing taste. Your canine is going to need less fat in his diet, so you should make healthier food choices while still considering the taste. These dietary changes will be different from the puppy and active adult foods you fed your Westie in the past.

Exercise

It's up to you to adjust your dog's schedule and to keep him less active yet happy. Shorter and more frequent walks should take care of your Westie's exercise needs, as well as helping to break up your day a little more.

Your dog will enjoy napping as much as walking, especially if he gets to cuddle with you. Sleeping beside you while you watch television or as you nap is pretty much all it takes to make your older Westie content!

You may notice your Westie spends more time sniffing during walks, which could be a sign that your dog is tiring. If he is walking slower, looking up at you, and flopping down, that could be his way of letting you know it's time to return home. If your canine can no longer manage long walks, make them shorter and more often. You could also spend more time romping around your yard or at home with your buddy.

Aging and the Senses

Just like people, dogs' senses weaken as they get older. They won't hear things as well as they used to, they won't see things as clearly, and their sense of smell will weaken.

The following are some of the signs your dog is losing at least one of his senses:

- It becomes easy to surprise or startle your dog. You need to be careful because this can make your Westie aggressive.
- Your dog may seem to ignore you or is less responsive when you issue a command.
- Cloudy eyes may be a sign of sight loss, though it does not mean your dog is blind.

If your aging dog seems to "behave badly," it is a sign that he is aging, not that he wants to rebel. Do not punish your older dog.

Adjust your schedule to meet your dog's changing abilities. Adjust his water bowl's height, refrain from rearranging rooms, and pet your dog more often. Make sure his bed is fluffy, or get him a new, more comfortable bed. Put the bed on the floor if it was previously kept on furniture. Your dog is probably nervous about losing his abilities, so it is up to you to comfort him.

Keeping Your Senior Dog Mentally Active

"I get a lot of questions from families with senior Westies asking if it's appropriate to add a Westie puppy to the mix. My answer is that it completely depends on your senior. Try him or her around a puppy and see how they do. If it seems to liven your senior up, a pup may add some fun and years onto your senior's life. However, if they're cranky toward a pup, give them space. Allow them to live out their golden years as the center of your universe and hold off on a pup until it works for everyone in your household."

FRANCES ROBERSON
Nancy's Westies

Just because your older Westie can't walk as far as he used to doesn't mean his brain is weaker too. As long as your Westie performs all of the basic commands, you can teach him all kinds of new, low-impact tricks.

At this point, training could be easier because your Westie has learned to focus better, and he'll be happy to have something he can still do with you. New toys are another fun way to help keep your dog's mind active. Be careful the toys aren't too rough on your dog's jaw and teeth. There are also food balls, puzzles, and other games that focus on cognitive abilities—and games such as hide and seek will still be very much appreciated!

Some senior dogs suffer from cognitive dysfunction syndrome (CCD), a type of dementia. It is estimated that 85% of all cases of dementia in dogs go undiagnosed because of the difficulty in pinpointing the problem. It manifests itself more as a problem of temperament than of cognitive ability.

If your dog begins to act differently, you should take him to the vet to see if he has CCD. While there really isn't any treatment for this problem, your vet can recommend things that will help your dog focus. An action such as rearranging the furniture is strongly discouraged because your dog relies on the familiarity of his surroundings to reduce his stress.

Mental stimulation at this time of your Westie's life is also still a must. Not only will keeping his mind active fight CCD, but it will also keep him healthy whether he exhibits signs of dementia or not.

Advantages to the Senior Years

The last years of your Westie's life can be just as enjoyable (if not more so) than the earlier stages since your dog has mellowed over time. All those high-energy activities will give way to relaxing and enjoying time with you. Your Westie will continue to be a loving companion, interacting with you at every opportunity. That does not change with age. However, your canine's limitations should dictate interactions and activities. If you are busy, make sure you schedule time with your Westie to do things that are within those limitations. It is just as easy to make an older Westie happy as it is to make a young dog happy!

Preparing to Say Goodbye

"When you begin with a young puppy the thought of losing him or her is far from your thoughts. But the reality exists. I used to think it was cruel that our four-legged furry friends lived such short lives in comparison to our own. I now believe that God places them in our hands to care for, love, and lose, in order to teach us how to handle the human loses in our lives."

BONNIE SUE HURLEY
OakTree Kennels

No pet parent wants to think about this last step, but as you watch your Westie slow down, you will know when your time with your sweet pup is coming to an end. Some dogs can continue to live for years after they begin to slow down, but many dogs don't make it more than a year or two. Sometimes dogs will lose their interest in eating, will have a stroke, or another problem will arise without warning. Eventually, it will be time to say goodbye, whether at home or at the vet's office. You need to be prepared.

Talk to your family about how you should care for your dog over the last few years or months of his life. Many dogs will be perfectly happy, continuing life as usual, despite their limited abilities. Some may begin to have problems controlling their bowel movements, while others may have problems getting up from a prone position. There are solutions to all of these problems. Always remember that quality of life should be your primary concern.

Since your dog cannot tell you how he feels, you must take cues from your Westie. If your dog still seems happy, there is no reason to have him euthanized.

FUN FACT
Longevity

West Highland White Terriers live an average of 12 to 15 years. A health survey completed in 2005 by the West Highland White Terrier Club of America determined that the average age of death out of 322 Westies surveyed was 11.4 years, with males living an average of 11.1 years and females living 11.7 years on average. The oldest dog who participated in the survey was 21.2 years old.

At this stage, your dog is probably happy just sleeping near you for eighteen hours a day. This is perfectly fine as long as he still gets excited about walking, eating, and being petted. The purpose of euthanasia is to reduce suffering, not to make things more convenient for yourself. This is what makes the decision so difficult, but your dog's behavior should be a fairly good indicator of how he is feeling. Here are some other things to watch when evaluating your dog's quality of life:

- Appetite
- Drinking
- Urinating and defecation
- Pain (noted by excessive panting)
- Stress levels
- Desire to be active or with family (If your dog wants to be alone most of the time, this is usually a sign he is trying to be alone for the end of his life.)

Talk to your vet if your dog has a serious illness to determine the best path forward. They can provide the best information on the quality of your dog's life and how long your dog is likely to live with his disease or ailment.

If your dog gets to the point where he is no longer happy, he can't move around, or he has a fatal illness, it is probably time to say goodbye. This is a decision that should be made as a family, always putting the dog's needs and quality of life first. If you decide it is time to say goodbye, determine who will be present at the end.

If you have decided to euthanize your dog, you can make his last few minutes calming and peaceful by feeding your dog the things he couldn't eat before. Foods like chocolate and grapes can put a smile on his face for his remaining time in your life.

You can also have your dog euthanized at home. If you decide to request a vet to come to your home, be prepared for additional charges for the home visit. You also need to determine where you want your dog to be, whether inside or outside, and in which room if you decide to do it inside.

Make sure at least one person he knows well is present so that your dog is not alone during the last few minutes of his life. You don't want your dog to die surrounded by strangers. The process is fairly peaceful, but your dog will probably be a little stressed. He will pass within a few minutes of the injection but continue to talk to him as his brain will continue to work even after his eyes close.

Once your dog is gone, you need to determine what to do with the body:

● Cremation is one of the most common ways of taking care of the body. You can request an urn or ask for a container for his ashes so you can scatter your dog's ashes over his favorite places. Make sure you don't spread his ashes in places where this action is not permitted. Private cremation is more expensive than communal cremation, but it means the only ashes you receive are from your dog. Communal cremation occurs when several pets are cremated together.

● Burial is the easiest method after your dog is euthanized and can be performed at your home. However, you need to check local regulations to be sure burying your dog on your property is legal. You also need to consider the soil; if your yard is rocky or sandy, that will create problems when trying to bury your pet. Also, don't bury your pet in a spot that is near a well that people use as a drinking source or if it is near wetlands or waterways. Your dog's body can contaminate the water as it decays. You can also look into a pet cemetery if there is one in your area.

Grief and Healing

Dogs become members of our families, so their passing can be incredibly difficult. People go through all of the same emotions and feelings of loss with a dog as they do with close friends and family. The absence of your dog's presence in your life is jarring, especially with such a loving, loyal dog like the Westie. It will feel weird not to have that presence by your side as you move around your home, and it will be a constant reminder of your loss. In the beginning, you and your family will probably feel considerable grief. Saying goodbye will be extremely difficult, so taking a couple of days off work is not a bad idea. While some people might say your Westie was "just a dog," you know better; it is okay to feel the pain and to grieve as you would for any lost loved one.

Losing your Westie is also going to create a substantial change in your schedule. It will likely take a while to become accustomed to the shift in your day-to-day life. Fight the urge to go out and get a new dog because you almost certainly will not be ready yet.

Everyone grieves differently, so allow yourself to grieve in a way that is healthy for you. Everyone in your family will feel the loss differently, too, so let them do the same. Some people don't require much time, while others can feel the loss for months. There is no timetable, so don't try to force it on yourself or on any member of your family.

Talk about how you would like to remember your pup. You can have a memorial for your lost pet, tell stories, or plant a tree in your dog's memory.

Try to return to your normal routine as much as possible if you have other pets. This can be both painful and helpful as your other pets will still need you just as much as when your Westie was alive. This is especially true of other dogs that have also lost their companion.

If you find grief is hindering your ability to function normally, seek professional help. If needed, you can search online to find support groups in your area to help you and your family, especially if this was your first dog. Sometimes it helps to talk about the loss so that you can begin to heal.

Made in the USA
Middletown, DE
07 December 2022

17478916R00110